bush s

Barbara Baynton was born in 1857 to Irish immigrant parents in Scone, New South Wales, and spent her childhood and youth in the area. After being deserted by her first husband with whom she had three children, Baynton moved to Sydney in 1887. She married the retired surgeon Dr Thomas Baynton in 1890 and during this period began to write newspaper articles and letters, poems and sketches, some of which were published in *The Bulletin*. The powerful and haunting stories of *Bush Studies*, first published in 1902 while Baynton was in London, have long been recognised as Australian classics.

After her husband's death in 1904, Baynton travelled between Australia and England, publishing the short novel *Human Toll* in 1907. In 1921 she married the fifth Lord Headley but they separated soon after. Barbara Baynton died in 1929.

bush studies

BARBARA BAYNTON

With an introduction by ELIZABETH WEBBY
and a memoir by H. B. GULLETT

Angus&Robertson
An imprint of HarperCollins*Publishers*

Angus&Robertson

An imprint of HarperCollins *Publishers*, Australia

First published in 1902.
First published in Australia by Angus&Robertson Publishers in 1965.
A&R paperback edition 1972, A&R Classics paperback edition 1980,
Arkon paperback edition 1983, reprinted in 1984.
Eden paperback edition 1989, A&R paperback edition 1990.
Imprint Classics edition published by Angus&Robertson in 1993.
Reprinted 1993, 1994.
This edition published by Angus&Robertson 1995.

HarperCollins*Publishers*
25 Ryde Road, Pymble, Sydney NSW 2073, Australia
31 View Road, Glenfield, Auckland 10, New Zealand
77–85 Fulham Palace Road, London W6 8JB, United Kingdom
Hazelton Lanes, 55 Avenue Road, Suite 2900, Toronto, Ontario, M5R 3L2
and 1995 Markham Road, Scarborough, Ontario, M1B 5M8, Canada
10 East 53rd Street, New York NY 10032, United States of America

National Library of Australia Cataloguing-in-Publication data:

Baynton, Barbara, 1857–1929.
  Bush studies.

  ISBN 0207 18948X
  I. Title.
A823.2

Cover illustration: *A Bush Burial* 1890
Frederick McCubbin, Australia
Collection: Geelong Art Gallery. Purchased by public subscription 1900.

Printed in Australia by Griffin Paperbacks

9 8 7 6 5 4 3 2 1
99 98 97 96 95

To
HELEN McMILLEN
of Sydney
New South Wales

CONTENTS

BUSH STUDIES

Introduction

In the memoir of his grandmother included in this edition of *Bush Studies,* H. B. Gullet observes that "she was a highly imaginative woman with no strict regard for the truth. She told her children many conflicting stories of her early years and of her parents, and it rather seems as if the truth to her was what she chose to believe it ought to be at any given moment. . . ." Research into Barbara Baynton's life, carried out since this memoir was written for the 1965 reprint of *Bush Studies,* has amply demonstrated the truth of his observation. Ironically, for a writer primarily praised for her realism, Baynton invented a highly romanticised version of her parentage, as well as understating her age by five years. She was born Barbara Jane Lawrence at Scone, a New South Wales country town, on 4 June 1857. Her parents, John Lawrence, a carpenter, and his wife, Elizabeth, née Ewart, had emigrated from Derry, Ireland, in 1840. Their backgrounds would appear to have been much less grand than the linen trade Baynton claimed for her purported mother, Penelope Ewart, and the military career she gave to her entirely fictional father, Captain Kilpatrick.

As Sally Krimmer and Alan Lawson note in their introduction to *Barbara Baynton* her "invention for her parents of a de facto relationship is difficult to comprehend in an era when public opinion and social standards made a respectable background so important. It may have been that in some of the bohemian circles in which she later moved her background was acceptable, romantically enviable. On the other hand her claim that her father was a landowner may have sounded more advantageous socially than his real occupation of carpenter.''[1] Perhaps, too, in inventing parents too passionately in love to abide by Victorian conventions, Barbara Baynton was compensating for what appear to have been three emotionally unsatisfactory marriages of her own. Each was, however, a distinct step upwards, socially and materially. Her first, to Alexander Frater, a selector, relieved her from the tedium and odium of working as a governess for his family, though the marriage ended in divorce when he ran off with another woman. Her second, to the seventy-year-old Thomas Baynton, brought her financial security, no small matter to someone who had just spent three years supporting herself and three children in Sydney via such stratagems as running a hat shop and selling Bibles door-to-door.[2] Her third, to the English Lord Headley, brought her a title but, as her grandson notes, was not a success — this time she was the one to leave.

The stories collected in *Bush Studies* were written during Barbara Baynton's second marriage; they were perhaps prompted by literary discussions with her husband's friends, and certainly made possible by her new-found leisure. But while Baynton may never have started writing without the stimulus and security of her second marriage, it was her earlier life in the bush that provided her material. The pain of rejection, of being a deserted wife, may be detected behind both ''Squeaker's Mate'', where the now useless, injured woman is replaced with a new mate, and ''Billy Skywonkie'', where the putative housekeeper is dismissed because she is unsuitable as a sexual partner. But Baynton's representation of the Australian bush as ''no place for a woman'' extends far beyond the merely personal. Her stories are set apart from those of her male contemporaries of the 1890s by the blackness of her portrait of life in the bush.

While Baynton is often listed among the early *Bulletin* short story writers, only one of her stories was ever published there, and that, as we shall see, appeared in an abbreviated version. Interestingly, the person responsible for cutting this story, *Bulletin* literary editor A. G. Stephens, wrote in a later review of *Bush Studies*: "... its truthful glimpses of Australian life, graphically expressed, could not (would not) have been printed in any Australian paper, though they rank highly as literature and are circulated widely in book form when issued by an English publisher. We are too mealy-mouthed (in print) and stuff far too much 'respectable' wadding in our ears." Stephens went on to single out Baynton's depiction of "the facts of life" as a major reason for the book's capacity to shock: "*Bush Studies,* written to the fact, stresses what may be called the predominantly obstetric quality of typical Bush life. This quality comes naturally: the increase of flocks and herds is the daily business, the source of living income. There is no prudish shame in referring to the accidents of begetting and birth: they form the staple conversation in many a home, and the children calmly discuss chances with their parents. Transference of ideas to the human species is easy; for apart from begetting and birth the Bush yields to many of its denizens little excitement, scanty diversion of monotonous occupation. So *Bush Studies* has already appeared 'shocking' to some city critics, smug in the solace of churches, and theatres, and 'down-the-harbour' picnics. But the thing goes on."[3]

Truly, the thing went on, though one might not think so from reading many nineteenth-century Australian writers. Baynton's "Bush Church", particularly in its portrait of midwife Jyne, locally known as "the Rabbit Ketcher", is an excellent illustration of Stephens's comments, though

Baynton's treatment of sexuality extends beyond the
obstetric. "Billy Skywonkie" depends on the clearly well-
known practice of acquiring a new mistress by advertising
for a "housekeeper". This euphemism, of course, goes back
to the early days of convict settlement; nor was the practice
later confined to the bush, as we see from Mary Helena
Fortune's 1871 sketch "The Spider and the Fly".[4] Mary
Fortune's image of the male as sexual predator is one also
found in several of Baynton's stories, especially "The
Chosen Vessel" which, even today, must rank as one of the
most telling exposés of the patriarchal double standard.

Barbara Baynton's decidedly unrosy studies of life in the
bush, particularly her stress on the crudity, cruelty and
crimes to which others turned a blind eye and her acknowledgment of the sexual, were clearly the main reasons why
her work was characterised as "realist" by A. G. Stephens
and other earlier critics. For nineteenth-century critics,
realism was usually more a matter of content than of form or
style. Writers were labelled "realists" if they dealt seriously
and sympathetically with working-class characters, if they
used local rather than exotic settings and concentrated on
scenes from contemporary life. It did not matter if their plots
were loaded with coincidence and contrivance or their tone
tended towards the sentimental. Some later critics, perhaps
in reaction against the earlier praise of Baynton as a realist,
have found her stories unnatural and artificial. Obviously,
they are clearly the product of the 1890s rather than the
1940s but, when judged alongside most others of their
period, can be seen to anticipate a number of later develop-
ments in short story writing, particularly the more dramatic
form of narration through the eyes of one or more of the
characters.

It is instructive to compare the title of Henry Lawson's
first major collection of stories, *While the Billy Boils* (1896),
with Baynton's. Lawson's, evoking a group of mates gathered
around a campfire, foregrounds the relationship between

narrator and listener. Nearly all his stories are told by
someone to someone else. Baynton's *Bush Studies,* however,
points to her more dramatic, and seemingly more objective,
narrative mode. The initial impression of the "starkly
realistic" nature of her work probably resulted in part from
her decision to dispense with the customary cosy relationship between storyteller and listener. In most of Baynton's
stories, her control of point of view effectively removes the
intervening presence of the narrator, making it seem as if the
stories just happen.

In "The Dreamer", for example, most of the narrative is
given through the eyes, the ears, and the other senses of the
central female character as she struggles through a stormy
night to reach her old home and her mother. Criticism of
this story as stylistically overwrought depends on a reading
of it as an attempt to realistically depict a bush journey. Most
commentators align this story with an Australian tradition of
hostility between (white) man and nature, without noting
that this tradition is rarely as strongly present in works by
women. One might, instead, contemplate the title. It must
primarily refer to the central character who, in a turmoil of
anxiety, guilt and fear, is mentally and emotionally closer to
the world of nightmare than to that of objective reality.
Clearly, she has not visited her mother for many years — she
is a stranger to the porter, who "knew everyone in the
district". We are not told why she has been so long estranged
from her mother, but the blame seems to be hers since she
sees her fight with the flooded creek as appropriate
expiation:

> Long ago she should have come to her old
> mother, and her heart gave a bound of savage
> rapture in thus giving the sweat of her body for
> the sin of her soul.

The house towards which she travels is "the home of her
girlhood", and there is a sense in which her journey is a

journey back to childhood. As she travels along the road she
relives the past and her perceptions are coloured by childish
fears and superstitions. Powerless as a child against the
swollen waters of the creek, she calls her "child-cry" and, at
the last moment, imagines she hears and is saved by her
mother's "sweet dream-voice".

It is left to the reader to decide just how to interpret this
episode. Certainly, when the woman eventually reaches
home she finds her mother dead, an event anticipated from
the beginning of the story but still having power to shock.
The fact that there is no one to meet the woman at the
station, the sound of the carpenter hammering the coffin,
and, in particular, the overflowing waterspout, all fore-
shadow the final discovery. The image of the water running
to waste — something no living bushwoman would permit
because water means life — is a good example of how
Baynton's intimate knowledge of the bush allows her to
focus on telling details, which function both realistically
and symbolically within her stories.

The final lines of "The Dreamer" — "The daughter parted
the curtains, and the light fell on the face of the sleeper who
would dream no dreams that night" — recall the ending of
Lawson's "His Father's Mate". In this story the prodigal son
returns home to find his father dead:

> "Father! Do you want another mate?"
> But the sleeper did not — at least, not in this
> world.[5]

Though the two stories are in most other respects very
dissimilar, Baynton did acknowledge a debt to Lawson,
saying in a 1920 interview: "I remember thinking, after
reading *While the Billy Boils,* that here for the first time a
man had shown that the Bush was worth writing about, and
it was a great encouragement to me when I started to write."[6]

Another point of similarity between Lawson and Baynton
is the view, presented in more than one of their stories, that a

dog can be a better and truer mate than a man. This is well demonstrated in the next two stories in *Bush Studies,* "Squeaker's Mate" and "Scrammy 'And". The title of "Squeaker's Mate" is heavily ironic. Squeaker's work-mate is his wife rather than another man, but in neither sense of the word "mate" — the Australian or the sexual — is he a good mate for her. Baynton establishes the nature of the relationship between this ill-matched couple right from the opening sentence:

> The woman carried the bag with the axe and
> maul and wedges; the man had the billy and clean
> tucker-bags; the cross-cut saw linked them.

In an earlier version of "Squeaker's Mate", this sentence does not appear.[7] Instead, there is a "half-time school-master" who spells out the meaning of the relationship as "a case of the reversal of sex, and she a physiological study".[8] The revised story makes this point much more dramatically and economically, again showing how Baynton's significant detail functions on both the realistic and symbolic planes. The woman is carrying the heavier work tools: she, as we see in the first page of the story, is the one who accepts responsibility, makes the decisions and does most of the hard work. Squeaker, an appropriately diminutive and demeaning name suggesting a mouse — or rat — fills the role usually assigned to women, carrying the food, and avoids work as much as possible. Significantly, the one thing that links them is a tool of separation.

"Squeaker's Mate" also provides a good illustration of how effectively Baynton can use a shifting point of view. After the first introductory paragraph, the point of view is that of the woman. But after the tree has fallen and injured her, the perspective is Squeaker's:

> He laid her on her back when he drew her out, and
> waited expecting some acknowledgment of his
> exertions, but she was silent, and as she did not

> notice that the axe, she had tried to save, lay with
> the fallen trunk across it, he told her. She cared
> almost tenderly for all their possessions and
> treated them as friends. But the half-buried
> broken axe did not affect her. He wondered a
> little, for only last week she had patiently
> chipped out the old broken head, and put in a
> new handle.

This not only makes more believable the woman's action in
trying to save the axe — "She cared almost tenderly"
suggesting that for this barren woman her possessions are
surrogate children — but stresses Squeaker's contrasting
callousness and imperception. As with the overflowing
water in "A Dreamer", the woman's lack of concern for her
tools is a sign that something is seriously wrong. So the
horror, and pathos, of her accident is conveyed much more
tellingly than if it had been presented in direct narrative.
When Red Bob and the other men come to the woman's
rescue the story reverts to direct narrative and alternates
between this and the woman's point of view until close to
the end. Through her eyes we see Squeaker letting the
selection go to ruin, neglecting the animals — not to
mention the woman herself — while he gallivants in town
spending her hard-earned money and, ultimate insult,
eventually returning with a new mate: a younger, pregnant
woman. Near the end of the story there is another effective
switch to the younger woman's point of view as, desperate
for water, she attempts to steal some from the injured
woman. This heightens the tension in preparation for the
climax of the story, where the older woman seizes the
younger in a vice-like grip: "As a wounded, robbed tigress
might hold and look, she held and looked." In the earlier
version of "Squeaker's Mate", the sexual jealousy made
obvious here was developed into a chilling ending. Dying,
Squeaker's mate hallucinates that a tree falls and crushes the

new mate; then she holds out her arms to Squeaker. The revised ending is more conventional, highlighting the dog, who prevents Squeaker touching the woman, as the only true mate.

In "Scrammy 'And"[9] the dog proves equally loyal, and even more human, with part of the story being told from his perspective. It opens with the focus on the dog's master, the misogynistic old shepherd, left alone to mind the selection while its owner takes his wife to town to have her baby. The shepherd is clearly to be seen as a bush type well known in nineteenth-century Australia: the hatter. This was a man, often an ex-convict, who preferred to live alone, working at a solitary occupation such as prospecting or shepherding. Hatters were popularly supposed to spend their spare time making cabbage-tree hats, as the old man does in this story. Lawson's "The Bush Undertaker" gives a quite similar picture of a hatter, though written in a much more comic mode.

There is, in fact, a good deal of humour in the opening section of "Scrammy 'And" as the old man talks to his dog, and as Baynton builds up the parallels between them. A darker note is, however, sounded almost from the beginning, as "the gloom of fear" settles on the old man's face, though he tries to persuade himself that Scrammy has left the selection. Again, a large part of the power of this story comes from Baynton's use of a shifting point of view. The first part of the story is told from the perspective of the old man. A shift to Scrammy's point of view effectively conceals the fact of the old man's death. A different sort of dog-and-man parallel is now set up, since both Scrammy and the dog are equally puzzled by the old man's silence. Eventually Scrammy — and the reader — discover the reason for this. The dog never does, leading to the horrific — horrific as much for what it does *not* say — ending as the selector and his wife return. The ending catches up with several earlier references to blowflies:

> The sight inside of that broken-ribbed dog's fight
> with those buzzing horrors, and the reproach in
> his wild eyes, was a memory that the man was not
> willing she should share.

"Billy Skywonkie" also makes good use of a limited point of view to keep vital information from the reader until later in the story. Structurally, "Billy Skywonkie" resembles "A Dreamer". Both depict difficult and ultimately pointless journeys made by solitary women. Both, after one or two introductory paragraphs, tell the rest of the story from the perspective of this central character. So the reader is uncertain about how much allowance to make for possible distortions in perception caused by the women's emotional states. In "Billy Skywonkie", however, a most important piece of information — that the woman is half-Chinese — is withheld until the second half of the story. This delayed explanation places the reader in a confusing situation of mystery, unreason and seemingly meaningless persecution.

Why does the bushman ignore the woman's questions? Why, when she leaves the train, is she subject to crude jokes and insults? Why does Billy Skywonkie almost drive off without her? Why does the Konk — himself such a grotesque specimen of humanity — stare at the woman as if there is something very wrong with her? Why does he refuse to give Billy the promised emu eggs? What is the significance of his reference to "Sally Ah Too"? All is explained when we learn that the woman is doubly marginalised within bush society.

"Billy Skywonkie", perhaps because it has been seen as primarily "comic" or "farcical", has received much less attention from critics and editors than either "Squeaker's Mate" or "The Chosen Vessel". Yet it has always seemed to me the most nightmarish of Baynton's stories and, in its subtle way, the most horrific. Here she exposes not only the sexual exploitation of women but the inherent racism of

Australian society. In both respects Barbara Baynton was a pioneer.

"Bush Church" is the only story in *Bush Studies* that could truly be described as a farcical comedy. The difference of tone is apparent from the aphoristic opening sentence: "The hospitality of the bush never extends to the loan of a good horse to an inexperienced rider." Unlike the other stories, "Bush Church" is not told from the point of view of one or more of its characters but is narrated by an urbane, amused and highly superior onlooker.

The parson's failure, at the beginning of the story, to control the horse, old Rosey, anticipates his later failure to control the attention of his congregation. Most of them, in fact, have only been induced to come by the misleading information that the parson is a government man, who may have them removed from their selections if they don't cooperate. Much of the humour derives from the very different expectations and assumptions of these poor selectors and those of the parson and the grazier's wife, at whose house the service is being held:

> A look of agony came into the eyes of the grazier's
> wife as she heard the door of the dining-room
> open. The children were so quiet, that she knew
> they were up to mischief.

Sure enough, they completely wreck the dinner she has prepared for the clergyman, leading to the wonderful ending with its return to the urbanity of the opening:

> At that moment Jinny, who had been awakened
> for the christening, looked around the door.
> "Our Sis wants ter know w'en's 'er supper's goin'
> ter be!" she said.
>   This perhaps was an acknowledgement that Sis
> had already dined.

The last story, "The Chosen Vessel", picks up themes of the
exploitation of women and of hypocritical double standards
from earlier stories and combines them with the subversive
questioning of the value of religion seen in "Bush Church".
A version of this story appeared in the *Bulletin* in December
1896 under the title "The Tramp". The section of the story
dealing with Peter Hennessey was omitted and there were
many other more minor differences from the story as
printed in *Bush Studies*. The cuts would appear to have been
made by A. G. Stephens, with Barbara Baynton's consent.[10]
The Peter Hennessey material and the present title first
appeared in a version of the story privately printed in
Sydney, as an undated pamphlet. Apart from one sentence,
the rest of the story was as printed in the *Bulletin*; it was
thoroughly revised before publication in *Bush Studies*.

One revised passage shows how Barbara Baynton
considerably sharpened her criticisms of male attitudes to
women and made clearer the sexual nature of the threat to
the woman alone in the hut. In both "The Tramp" and the
pamphlet version of "The Chosen Vessel", the woman does
not go off to her absent husband because "as yet she had not
set her will against his as with the cow, and so dared not". In
the 1902 version of the story, this is replaced by:

> But in the past, when she had dared to speak of
> the dangers to which her loneliness exposed her,
> he had taunted and sneered at her. She need not
> flatter herself, he had coarsely told her, that
> anybody would want to run away with her.

In a final revision for the 1917 edition of *Bush Studies,* the
last sentence was given as direct speech, making it even
more emphatic.

Several critics have expressed a preference for "The
Tramp" over "The Chosen Vessel", seeing the Peter
Hennessey section as an unnecessary encumbrance on an
otherwise taut tale of terror. But this section of the story acts

as an ironic counterpoint to the main episode of rape and murder, extending its meaning from an account of a particular crime to a general reflection on male attitudes to women.[11] As this section and the second title indicate, women can be "chosen vessels" in both the highest sense — as the Virgin Mother, chosen by God to bring Christ into the world — and the lowest — as rape victims, chosen as the objects of male lust and violence. That Baynton is primarily concerned here to expose the patriarchal double standard which treats women as "the Other" — objects to be either worshipped or abused — is apparent from the beginning of the story where the woman's husband forces her to confront the cow and laughs at her terror. A. A. Phillips claimed there was no need for the husband to appear in the story.[12] But the callous husband is necessary not only thematically but in terms of the plot: as indicated above, the woman fears her husband even more than she fears the swagman.

As reviews by A. G. Stephens and others testify, *Bush Studies* was published to considerable critical acclaim. But critical interest in Baynton's work was not sustained, and her stories were for many years out of print. Though *Bush Studies* has been readily available since 1965, there is still relatively little written on Baynton's stories, most of it dating from the 1980s.[13] Failure to acknowledge earlier the significance of Barbara Baynton's contribution to Australian literature may in part be attributed to the comparative shortness of her writing life and smallness of her output. Besides the six stories included in *Bush Studies,* she published only three further stories, a novel, *Human Toll* (1907), ten poems and three brief articles. But one cannot help feeling that past promoters of Australian literature and the Australian tradition have been somewhat discomforted by Barbara Baynton's less than flattering descriptions of bush life, and of its male inhabitants in particular.

ELIZABETH WEBBY
University of Sydney

Notes

1. Sally Krimmer and Alan Lawson, *Barbara Baynton* (University of Queensland Press, 1980), p. xi. Baynton's great-granddaughter, Penne Hackforth-Jones claims, however, in her biography *Barbara Baynton: Between Two Worlds* (Penguin, 1989) that Baynton's parents were living in a de facto relationship at the time of her birth and that her father's real name was Robert Kilpatrick, though he was a carpenter rather that a soldier and landowner (pp. 6–7).

2. See Patricia Clarke, *Pen Portraits. Women writers and journalists of nineteenth century Australia* (Allen & Unwin, 1988), p. 140.

3. The *Bulletin*, 28 February 1903. Reprinted in Leon Cantrell (ed.), *A. G. Stephens: Selected Writing* (Angus & Robertson, 1977), pp. 202–203.

4. Originally published in the *Australian Journal*: reprinted in Fiona Giles (ed.), *From the Verandah* (McPhee Gribble/Penguin, 1987), pp. 53–60.

5. Colin Roderick (ed.), *Henry Lawson, Short Stories and Sketches, 1888–1922* (Angus & Robertson, 1972), p. 10.

6. Originally published in *Home*; reprinted in Krimmer and Lawson, op. cit., p. 327.

7. Manuscript in the Mitchell Library; reprinted in Elizabeth Webby, "Barbara Baynton's Revisions to 'Squeaker's Mate' ", *Southerly*, 44, 1984, pp. 455–68.

8. Elizabeth Webby, op. cit.

9. The title comes from the nickname of one of the characters, referring to the fact that he has a maimed or defective hand. See G. A. Wilkes, *A Dictionary of Australian Colloquialisms* (Sydney University Press, 1978), p. 285.

10. See Krimmer and Lawson, op. cit. p. 3.

11. See Kay Iseman, "Barbara Baynton: Woman as 'The Chosen Vessel' ", *Australian Literary Studies,* 11, 1983, pp. 25–37.

12. "Barbara Baynton and the Dissidence of the Nineties", *The Australian Tradition* (Cheshire-Lansdowne, 1966), pp. 74–5.

FURTHER READING
Additional studies of Barbara Baynton's stories include:

Thea Astley, "The Teeth Father Naked at Last: The short stories of Barbara Baynton", *Three Australian Writers* (Townsville Foundation for Australian Literary Studies, 1979), pp. 12–22.

Lucy Frost, "Barbara Baynton: An Affinity with Pain", in Shirley Walker (ed.), *Who Is She? Images of Women in Australian Fiction* (University of Queensland Press, 1983), pp. 56–70.

Rosemary Moore, " 'Squeaker's Mate': A Bushwoman's Tale", *Australian Feminist Studies*, 3, 1986, pp. 27–44.

Kay Schaffer, *Women and the Bush: Forces of Desire in the Australian Cultural Tradition* (Cambridge University Press, 1988).

MEMOIR
OF
BARBARA BAYNTON

Memoir
of Barbara Baynton

W RITERS OF FICTION are generally only convincing when
the subject of their work falls within their personal experience; and so it follows that the life of an author is of interest
primarily because it dictates the limits and character of what
is written.

Barbara Baynton, my grandmother, published only two
books and they were concerned exclusively with the obser-
vations of her childhood and her youth. She wrote *Bush
Studies* in her early and middle thirties by which time, as
we shall see, she had had a wide experience of life and had
acquired a maturity unusual in her years.

From many points of view, then, it would seem sufficient,
in a biographical outline written to preface the republishing
of her short stories, merely to give some account of her life
to the point when she completed this work. But her publishers have suggested, and I agree, that there is merit in
outlining the whole of her life. We take this view not only
because we believe her background and life were sufficiently

unusual as to be worthy of attention in themselves, but also because of the increasing interest which Australians of today feel in those years of their country's development, when so much of our national character first began to take shape and to find expression.

For these were the years when through the eyes of our own native-born we first began to see our country in a realistic perspective. Australia was no longer merely a outpost extension of Britain which was, of course, the real centre of the universe and civilized life—home. "Home", reality, the surge of life, was right here in Sydney Town, out on the Castlereagh, up on the Monaro. In a fever of energy and with astounding confidence, this generation thrust their roots down, tore into the forests and the quarries. In a few decades they transformed Sydney and Melbourne from shanty towns to cities in their own right —solid, even pretentious, built to last. If oak and daffodil would not grow, eucalypt, wattle and Norfolk pine would. If they could not paint the heavy golden vapour-light of England, they would paint something clearer, harsher, something that had meaning and was of them. It was no longer what Mr Gladstone had said six months ago, but what Henry Parkes said yesterday which counted now. So with their writers. No more of these "accounts" of this and that, these patronizing epistles of visitors writing from the outside. Australian writing would be by Australians, written from the inside and with the insight that comes only from this perspective. And they would write, too, not of a self-consciously respectable middle-class society, but of that section of the people which was the most dramatic because it was the most unusual: the station-hand, the ganger, the half-caste, the convict, the remittance man, the drover's wife, the bushranger.

So it was with my grandmother.

It is not easy to give a factual account of her life. She

was born over a hundred years ago and the difficulties of reproducing the atmosphere in which she grew up are obvious. No one is now alive who knew her in her vital attractive youth, and few who remember her turbulent middle age. The recollection of her as an elderly, eccentric, and most difficult woman, is as a general portrait, and, for our purpose, neither useful nor fair. Again, she was a highly imaginative woman with no strict regard for truth. She told her children many conflicting stories of her early years and of her parents, and it rather seems as if the truth to her was what she chose to believe it ought to be at any given moment, and of course it would vary with her moods.

It is inevitable that this account of her, then, will contain minor inaccuracies, but it is substantially correct, and the impression I have given of her is as accurate as I can make it.

Since Elizabethan times, the principal cities of Northern Ireland, Belfast and Londonderry, have been occupied in the manufacture of linen. In this trade the family of Ewart has been a leading one for several centuries. About 1855, a younger son of this merchant house, Robert Ewart, married one of his cousins, Penelope Ewart. She had no fortune, and, as her husband was considered delicate, his family decided to do with advantage as they had often done before with younger sons—send them out to the colonies to establish yet another outlet for their linen products. The young couple were by no means well-off, yet they brought with them, in addition to the means of setting up in business, a few nice pieces of china, silver, and furniture. The ship called at Bombay and took on, among other passengers, a Captain Kilpatrick, formerly of the Bengal Light Cavalry. This was in the year 1858 and there is reason to believe that Kilpatrick's first wife had perished in the Mutiny the year before. I have a daguerreotype of Captain Kilpatrick about

this time; he was a handsome man and something of a
dandy if one is to judge by the rings, waistcoat buttons,
and other jewellery which he left. Robert Ewart, being far
from robust, spent a good deal of time in his cabin. His
bride, on the other hand, was always in splendid health
and so, apparently, was Captain Kilpatrick. They saw a
great deal of each other. It is a familiar enough shipboard
story and one probably more common in the days of slow
ships and tedious passages. But their relationship did not
end with the termination of the voyage, and soon after the
ship's arrival in Sydney, Mrs Ewart left her husband for
Captain Kilpatrick. Now the consequences of this sort of
behaviour have always been difficult to avoid and as a rule
only two classes of people have succeeded in doing so—
the wealthy and powerful, whom society has to recognize,
and the very poor who don't give a damn. Mrs Ewart
belonged to neither category. Moreover, she came of that
inflexible Presbyterian Scottish stock, which makes it a
certainty that she had been brought up with the strictest
attention to the proprieties. For the rest of her days she
led a life of impeccable rectitude. Her action she must have
well known was both scandalous and, by her lights, wicked.
Short of marrying a Papist she could hardly have committed
a more wilful or self-destructive action. However, off she
went. She must have been deeply infatuated with Captain
Kilpatrick, and she must also have been a person of the
greatest resolution

For this alliance clearly posed most formidable problems
for the Kilpatricks, as they were now known. They may
have imagined that they could "get away with it" in the
colonies. But in a Sydney increasingly conscious of its newly
established respectability, they would have soon been disil-
lusioned. Their action had indeed placed them outside
decent society, and they had henceforth to live literally
beyond its pale. There is no record of Kilpatrick's having

obtained a grant of land or any particular reason why he should have done so. On the contrary. Such grants, in any case, usually went to men of means or influence, and men of means did not enter the forces of the East India Company, even though it was, in itself, a lucrative if uncertain profession. I think it likely that he became a station manager. He belonged to what one might call the authoritative classes, and he would have had a good knowledge of men and horses and, of course, "natives". At all events, they lived up in the Castlereagh district, and there their children were born, my grandmother being the youngest of six.

The impressions I have of her childhood are to some extent based on the things my grandmother herself told me and my sister, but far more upon the stories my mother passed on to us. Mrs Kilpatrick lived to a fairly considerable age and my mother spent a good deal of time with her and so she had a good deal at first hand.

The Castlereagh had at this time been settled—perhaps occupied is a better word—for the best part of a generation. One imagines extremely primitive though not altogether uncomfortable conditions. Although people were far more class-conscious in those days, yet a consideration of any of the older homesteads makes it clear that these rural communities lived in far closer proximity than is the case today. Into these rambling though not very extensive homes were crammed large families of children, domestic servants and their offspring, and within a stone's throw there were huts for workmen of various kinds. For obvious reasons far more labour was required than is the case today. A station or large farm was a considerable settlement, complete and self-sufficient to a degree found today only in the largest stations with their gardens, workshops, forge, store, butcher's "shop", and so on.

To judge by the vigorous children this generation produced it is clear they did not lack the basic essentials;

yet life had little of elegance. There would not have been much to attract the Kilpatricks in their new way of life, but a great deal to horrify and repel them. I do not doubt they saw this country as the enemy, and life a ceaseless battle to retain the basic decencies. Mrs Kilpatrick would have missed the trim orderliness, the decent seemliness of Presbyterian Ulster; Kilpatrick would have been shocked by the roughness and brutality of this unsoldierly disorder.

I imagine this somewhat cultivated but harsh man constantly at war with his environment, a war mainly for his children and one in which the odds were too strong for him. For the people among whom he now lived were, for one reason and another, like himself—outcasts from society. Here were time-expired convicts, ticket-of-leave men, drunkards, degenerates, half-castes, blacks. Worse, there was a rising generation which knew no other life, and of this generation were his children.

But however much they may have disliked it the Kilpatricks had set their foot to this road and they had to tread it. They turned for protection to themselves, and to each other, and here they found strength. They were an almost excessively devoted couple, and, as is not infrequent with such *ménages*, they were indifferent parents. Like many middle-class migrants they developed into severe and unbending autocrats. Though they failed to force their standards on to their children, yet in their presence at least were decency, obedience, fear, the Presbyterian religion. Mrs Kilpatrick had a tongue like a whip-lash and she used it unsparingly on her servants, her children and her neighbours. Kilpatrick was aloof and stern. Each supported the other absolutely.

Though she turned a proud, high face to the world, Mrs Kilpatrick never lost her sense of guilt and regarded her harsh life as a sort of judgement for her behaviour. It could not have been a very happy household.

I have implied that they were not primarily interested in their children. These would grow up no better than their neighbours, but to this there was only one exception —their youngest daughter, Barbara. Three years before this child was born, Robert Ewart died in Sydney. He was buried at the old cemetery where Central Station now stands, and he never recovered from his wife's desertion for on his tombstone was engraved, in the manner of the time, "He died of a broken heart." The Kilpatricks were now married and their subsequent children born in wedlock. But for Mrs Kilpatrick the sense of guilt remained, and for both of them the price had still to be paid.

Barbara grew into a good-looking and gifted young woman and so it was reasonable to assume that she was an attractive child. At any rate, she was certainly the favourite of both her parents. She associated with them more than her brothers and sisters did and she was more influenced by their attitudes. From her mother she had a strong religious sense; from her father, something of his authoritative outlook and bearing. She also read his books. From these there is no evidence to show that Kilpatrick was a scholar, but he read a good deal. Rather surprisingly he liked Dickens, and he bought other novels currently appearing at the time, especially the Russians. He didn't care for romances, he preferred—as I have said—the Russians, Tolstoy, Dostoevsky, Turgenev; also Edgar Allan Poe.

When she was about fourteen, Barbara developed an eye infection, loosely known as sandy blight. It left her eyes greatly weakened. Her long sight was always good, but for the rest of her life she was able to read only by holding the book two or three inches from her face. From this time on in fact, she read very few new books. She did not wish, she used to say, "to use up my eyes on rubbish". It is interesting, I think, to see what she did read. First of all, and most thoroughly, the Bible, at the behest of her mother,

still turning the knife—"Thou shalt not commit adultery";
Dickens was always a favourite, and the Russians. I
remember her saying, "The Russians are always doing something. They write about love and death, and war and
violence—not about infantile romances and tea parties."

And so we see her growing up with a foot in both worlds:
her parents', with something of refinement and a connection with the outside world in their books, in their few
pieces of silver and china and jewellery which they had
brought with them; and the other, the new life of a distant
bush settlement, with all its harshness and cruelty, with
black and white, bond and free, oaf and gentleman, still
in the melting pot, striving and stirring with all the force
and passion of a primitive society. She was at home in both
worlds and yet, I think, belonged entirely to neither. One
sees her with her brothers and companions, bringing with
her a gift for pointed expression, for ridicule, for making
people laugh; at ease with them, always sought-after as an
amusing and an imaginative companion, yet by virtue of
these very qualities a little removed from them. She saw
and understood them from the inside, for she had been
born to it, but the eyes she saw them with were not their
eyes.

When she was about eighteen Barbara married Robert
Frater, a grazier of Scots descent from the Scone district,
where she lived for seven or eight years. There her two
sons and daughter were born. I have a photograph taken of
her at this time in Sydney. She has a broad clear brow,
her eyes very dark, long, and widely spaced. Her mouth
also is rather wide, well-shaped and mobile, her chin short
and pointed. Her hair is brown and very thick, her eye-
brows rather strongly marked. The planes of her face are
too flat for the idea of beauty at that time, but they gave
her certain distinction and they wore well. She was little
above the average height, but seemed taller as she always

stood very straight. Writing of her as she was in 1907, Vance Palmer remembers her as a large and generous figure, but she was never stout. Rather broad-shouldered she was, the waist and hips very small, beautiful hands, ankles and feet. She laughed a great deal and was extremely observant in the Dickens manner and so made others laugh pretty well as she wished. With her own splendid physical and mental equipment, she had no tolerance for the imperfections of others. Though many people found her sympathetic, she was curiously insensitive. Interested in other people, yet she cared very little for their welfare. She had not the faintest desire to reform or improve. People amused her, aroused her compassion or contempt, seldom her affection. Perhaps this is why her husband left her. At all events, leave her he did, for one of her own cousins who was at the time staying with her in their house.

The role of the deserted wife is never easy. It was much less so in Victorian times. To begin with, divorce was a slow and difficult process and in all cases damaging to the reputation. Barbara reacted to her situation with the vigour and decision typical of her. She raised what money she could on her husband's property and took her children to Sydney where she acquired a house in Ashfield. Divorce proceedings she began at once.

She seems to have had enough to live on, but from what source I do not know. But we do know that she had difficulty in controlling her sons and gradually lost interest in them, giving her affection, as her mother had done, almost entirely to her little daughter, Penelope. It is clear that the relationship between mother and daughter had a very special significance for her, as we see in her stories.

But fundamentally, and as always, she was interested in herself, and one is tempted to wonder if she did not, despite its wounding and humiliating circumstances, welcome the event which had given her a degree of freedom so complete and so unusual at that period. She appears to have wasted very little time in regrets for her former life. The world was a wonderful place if you were young and attractive and sure of yourself, and even more wonderful if, in addition, you are rich and famous. Very good, she would be rich and famous, too. But how? She would be a singer. But she had just a voice—it wasn't enough. She would be a famous actress; and here she was nearer the mark, but there was one fatal drawback. Approaching thirty she was getting a little old to start. She would write, then; and she began immediately.

What she wrote I don't know, but her children always remembered her as writing. Certainly she wrote a few newspaper articles and letters, poems, and what at that time were called sketches. Some of these appeared in the *Bulletin* under her own name and I imagine there were other contributions which were rejected or which she did not sign. Poetry always appealed to her and she would have liked to have been able to write better poetry than she did. As it was, she had the perception to realize her limitations and concentrated on her prose writing. She was always a perfectionist. She wrote a piece again and again until satisfied she could not do it any better. But she was learning her trade, not doubting—one may be sure—that she would excel in it.

She had a large circle of acquaintances, and made many friends, among them a certain Dr Thomas Baynton. This Dr Baynton was son of an early Victorian settler who took up land near Kyneton. His people were, to use the terms of the day, English landed gentry, and when one of their sons had the folly to marry the local innkeeper's daughter, they packed him off to Australia. He built a substantial house near Kyneton and developed a very fine station. His son, Thomas, completed his education in England and became a doctor of medicine at Edinburgh. Life at Kyneton seems not to have attracted him and so he settled in Sydney. He did not practise medicine because he did not need to. He seems to have been a scholarly sort of man, dilettante and rather unworldly. It is easy to understand Barbara's attraction for him. For his part, though no longer young, Dr Baynton had a good deal to offer. He was comfortably off, educated, a gentleman, and he was prepared to take on the children. My grandmother spoke of him always with affection and respect, especially the latter. He was a typical pater familias of the period, devoted to his wife, severe with his step-sons, indulgent to his step-daughter. They had no other children.

The Bayntons had a house in Edgecliff, just off Ocean Street, and there Barbara passed seven or eight very happy years. She had an assured position, a pleasant house, and was able, within limits, to indulge her increasing taste for old and beautiful things. Dr Baynton had some fine Georgian silver, and my grandmother soon acquired more. We ourselves live in an age of uncritical veneration for the antique, an attitude for which my grandmother would have had nothing but contempt. Most of the things found in antique shops today are early Victorian or at best Regency. These were of course the modern idea in that period of her life of which I write. She thought them cumbersome, ugly and ill-made—"Victorian rubbish". Her interest in the antique sprang from her intense dislike for the contemporary. As her collection increased, so, of course, did her taste widen, and moved from the essentially elegant balanced style of the Georgian period to the more opulent Queen Anne and its French contemporary. In her later houses the living-rooms were principally Queen Anne though her dining-rooms were always Georgian, and it was this period which gave her the greatest pleasure. She was a possessive woman; yet though she knew a good picture when she saw one, she seldom bought it. She wanted to own things, to have the best, and she knew she would never be able to afford the best in pictures. But old silver or furniture or porcelain were quite another matter. In the then ruling prices she could afford to bid up with anyone and she did so.

Her circle was now largely her husband's; academics, professional men and "dabblers" in literature and the arts. As always she wished to impress herself upon it. At this time she began writing on the stories in *Bush Studies*. Writing does not seem to have come easily to her, she worked very hard, cutting and polishing, mostly in the afternoons. She was perhaps five years on *Bush Studies*, a long time for so short a work. But she lived a fairly full life, had a house to run, and her children must have made some demands upon her. In 1900 her second son went away to the South African War as a trooper. He was only fifteen, but she made no move to stop him. While he was away Dr Baynton died and his widow was left comparatively well off.

Many years later she used to take me with her on her drives round Sydney. In her early days there she had come to know it extremely well and to love it not only for its natural charm but for its old buildings, its unevenness, its unexpected and delightful views. And she had loved it too for its people. She had always the ability—though in later years she often lacked the desire—to put people of varied ages and classes at their ease. Her "bearing", to use the phrase of the day, was such that no one was likely to take a liberty with her so she had no need to be pompous or reserved. She liked people to talk and preferably to make fools of themselves, but she never let them know it and had the gift of leaving people feeling they were wiser, wittier, than they had previously thought. In short she believed like Pope that "the proper study of mankind is man", though that is not to say that she felt particular affection for mankind. Affection she had, but for a very few and these did not by any means include all her children or her brothers and sisters. For the vast majority then of her acquaintances she felt intense interest and a good deal of tolerance, not more. She spoke to every one she met as to an equal, at least as a human being, entitled to certain human dignities and rights including that of going to hell in their own particular way. She enjoyed her drives no end and so did I, largely because of the ridiculous stories of people which the once familiar scenes would recall to her.

Bush Studies was now almost finished. She could say that it was good, or as good as she could make it, taking into account the manner of writing of the day and the relatively few models which she had to guide her. For no work of fiction is entirely original. The creative instinct or ability must be there, but all writers are conditioned by what they themselves have read and absorbed from others. Barbara Baynton's writing shows very clearly what I might call her "root sources". Her powers of observation were her own, but sharpened by Dickens. Like the Russians she was never absorbed with trivia; the major passions, and only they, engrossed her. She never baulked at horror and, as de Maupassant did, she knew how to use suspense. Then work and work to give point, finality, and roundness. She shows, too, the faults of her sources, especially in her novel *Human Toll* when, like so many of her contemporaries, she piles on the agony and slips from sentiment to bathos.

With Dr Baynton's estate my grandmother was free to do pretty well as she chose. Among her friends were a number interested in business and finance, particularly the brothers Ernest and Arthur Hayes. They were New Zealanders, of ample means, and, acting on Ernest Hayes's advice, she began to invest in the Stock Exchange. She had an astute business instinct and was never averse to seeking advice from people qualified to give it. She was a very bold investor. The market had not yet recovered from the slump of the nineties, but confidence in the young colony was in the air, so she did very well. About 1903 she decided she could afford to go to England, probably encouraged by the reports which Duckworth's—the publishers—had written her on her manuscripts for *Bush Studies*. Penelope went with her. They were back, I think, in London when the book came out. It had a modest success. She did not make much money, but derived a good deal of pleasure from the flattering reception which it generally enjoyed with the critics. She was, in a modest way and in literary circles, something of a celebrity, not only because her work was good and because its subject-matter was entirely new to the English reader, but also because she herself was now a striking personality. Between 1905 and 1913 her fortunes prospered increasingly. These indeed were her golden years. She looked much younger than her age, always felt well and in excellent spirits. She had a succession of increasingly fine houses and here she surrounded herself with Dresden and Sevres and Chelsea, with silver and Battersea boxes, and Chippendale mahogany and Chinese lacquer. She dressed splendidly and wore beautiful jewellery. She had immense vitality, and, though her sallies made enemies, she gave great entertainment and had many friends and acquaintances. Her powers to impress and charm were very considerable. She met people not only at parties and receptions, but in railway trains, on the Continent, in antique shops and art galleries. She was asked to stay in great country houses and knew many people of rank and influence. In writing this I am not unaware that much of it sounds snobbish and pretentious, but it was after all my grandmother's point of view, and whatever this egalitarian age may think of it, these were the important factors of life in her time, and I know of no other way in which to describe them. This sort of !ife then completely absorbed if it did not satisfy her. Soon after the publication of *Bush Studies* she was encouraged to write *Human Toll*. This novel, like the short stories, was based on the experience of her youth, but she had really lost something of the urge to write, even the reason for writing. She had written for a definite purpose—to make a name for herself—and this she had done. It had enabled her to embark upon the life she had wanted. Now she was absorbed in living her life, not writing about it. *Human Toll* was her last sustained literary effort. She never worked as hard at this book as she had at *Bush Studies* and this is obvious. She had too many distractions, and probably, I think, she tired of it. There are some remarkably fresh passages in *Human Toll* and her understanding of children was considerable, clear, amused, and strangely modern in its freedom from illusion or inhibition. But the book was not the work of a literary craftsman and she knew it. Once *Human Toll* was finished she seldom referred to it. Indeed, she referred very little to *Bush Studies* either. Though not by any means a modest woman, she seldom alluded to the fact that she had written anything and for years before she died most of those who knew her were quite unaware she had done so. But her book was seldom far from her; she often read it and I see her putting it down with her wide cynical smile as if to say, "You may not care for it, but it's not too bad—do better yourself!"

She bought a lot of books but read very few of them. Most modern writers she held in the deepest contempt. She had an unerring eye for the involved sentence, for the loose and foolish statement. "My God!" she would say, "Listen to this!" . . . and she would read a piece of rubbish with the most malicious enjoyment. Before the first war she made several trips to Australia. She began buying black opals from Lightning Ridge and had one of the finest collections in the world. Her daughter married in 1911,

and Barbara missed her sorely. Her friends were getting
older now, as she was. The best of it indeed was over.
She was in England during the years of the first war, and
the sight of her fellow countrymen gave her immense pride.
She was not over fond of giving, but gave generously to
Australian servicemen's clubs and centres. Both her sons
served with the British and both were severely wounded,
and they brought many of their friends to their mother's
home in Great Cumberland Place. But she liked best to
have Australian soldiers, particularly young men from the
bush. She talked the language. As she grew older, too, she
valued more highly the standards of her youth. She admired
her countrymen because they were well-built, and strong
and brave, and so many of them good-looking. She cared
nothing that some of them got drunk and picked up tarts
and brawled with the authorities. Following some criticism
of the behaviour of Australian troops on leave in London
she wrote a most violent letter to *The Times*, defending
their right to do exactly as they pleased.

Another man who spoke her language was W. M. "Billy"
Hughes, Australia's wartime Prime Minister, who was a
great deal in London at this time. He was a prince of
story-tellers and a master of nonsense. Not long before he
died he said to me, "I used to go a lot to your grandmother's house—a remarkable woman. My God, she used
to make me laugh! But you know you never wanted to
argue with her. I haven't a very good reputation myself
when it comes to verbal disagreement, but Barbara—she
was bloody well impossible!" And this was true, for though
she had a rather masculine intelligence, she never hesitated
to use a woman's subterfuges. Once my mother said to
her, "I think you are rather unreasonable with old so-and-
so." And she replied, "My dear, unreason is a woman's
greatest weapon!"

Soon after the war she married Lord Headley. She liked the idea of a title, and no doubt Lord Headley liked the idea of a wealthy wife. Besides, they were old friends and had a good deal in common. Lord Headley was an eccentric in his own right and possessed a variety of talents. Though he had inherited estates in Ireland, as a young man he became a civil engineer, in which profession he achieved great distinction. Much of his life was spent building dams in Egypt and India and during this service he became a convert to Islam. He was a famous athlete until almost middle age, and a well-known sportsman of the hunting and shooting variety. Lord Headley was a fine-looking old man, not tall but robust and commanding with impressive white moustaches. About the time he married my grandmother the throne of Albania had become vacant and the leaders of that country, looking round for a king, had decided to offer him the job. He was of noble birth, a Muslim, a sportsman, and a gentleman. But the old boy, checking the available statistics, decided the kingship business, at least in Albania, had very little future and, to my grandmother's scorn, rejected the offer. Those who knew her considered Albania had had a most fortunate escape. As a consolation prize, certain notables of that country then gave my grandmother a fine blue sapphire brooch. They asked her to say frankly if she liked it. This was a mistake. She replied with fulsome thanks but added that, since they asked her, she in fact already possessed a blue sapphire brooch. She would, therefore, prefer a brown sapphire. Brown sapphires are generally more prized than blue ones but eventually a magnificent stone was duly found, set, and presented. One cannot help imagining that the departing Albanians felt thankful they were not to suffer my grandmother's closer acquaintance.

The marriage with Lord Headley was not a success. Barbara enjoyed her title and made haste to have her coronet engraved on her silver but had the good sense to except her oldest and finest pieces. But she was, by now, incapable of rearranging her life to suit the requirements of a sporting country gentleman, and to be fair to Lord Headley I do not think she made the slightest attempt to do so.

In fact she was becoming increasingly restless and hard to please. After a few years they parted.

I have said my grandmother wrote no more after *Human Toll*. This is not quite true. In 1920 she wrote two more short stories to be added to *Bush Studies*, but they are not generally considered to be of the same standard. She also wrote a number of stories to amuse her grandchildren. They were about the creatures of a farmyard, mostly chickens and a fox, a rat, a snake, a crow and other symbols of human unpleasantness and folly. They were in the classic tradition of English and German children's stories, which is to say they were satirical, sophisticated, and light-heartedly bloodthirsty. We adored them and I remember yet the wonderful mixture of fear and delight with which we listened to her read them. My mother tried very hard to persuade her to publish these stories but she would not, and I think perhaps she was wise.

For the remainder of her life, she lived alternatively in London and in Melbourne where she built a house in Toorak. It was furnished in a style calculated to impress the locals and it did. But after a year or so she became bored with it and sold everything in it except certain pieces of silver and porcelain of which she was very fond. Her things brought enormous prices and this so delighted her that she straight away returned to England and brought another shipload. This buying and selling gave her immense interest and pleasure. It is probably true to say my grand-mother brought more really first-class pieces of furniture and silver to this country than anyone has ever done not excluding dealers. She was perhaps the finest judge of furniture I have met and though, like all collectors, she made mistakes, she profited by them and never fooled herself though she was quite willing to fool others. Her second husband, Dr Baynton, was a useful wood-carver and cabinet-maker, and she learned from him the fundamentals of furniture construction and knew exactly how Chippendale furniture should be jointed; what timbers should be used in various parts of, say, a desk, how Sheraton applied his veneers, and so on. She had a very complete knowledge of the decorative styles of the great furniture makers and could tell you, for example, that the curving of the arms of such a chair were slightly out of character for the period—probably a French influence—perhaps a Huguenot craftsman, because this was a French way of doing it as you could see by these chairs over here, or "at least you could if you had eyes in your head, boy".

Her taste in porcelain was less sure. She had some beautiful pieces but except for a few personal things about her bedroom or desk, she inclined to opulence and display. Thus she had relatively little of the lovely and rather simple porcelain produced at Chelsea and Bow, but a good deal of Sèvres and Worcester and Derby.

In general her homes were over-crowded and the effect was not, perhaps, aesthetically pleasing, but it was fascinating; antique clocks, musical boxes, enamels, miniatures, ivories and jades, carvings and tapestries.

Sir John Longstaff painted her about this time. It makes an interesting and perhaps unhappy comparison with the photograph of the simply dressed young woman of forty years before. She is as one might say—in this portrait—in full battle order. On her grey hair is an opal tiara; she wears a dog-collar of pearls and then a very large single rope of very large pearls reaching almost to her waist. Her famous opal brooch, pearl earrings, bracelets and rings, complete her jewellery. She has a dark silk dress with sequins, black stockings and shoes. It is quite an outfit. At sixty she is still erect and robust, but the contours and expressions of her face are greatly changed. It is very much a grande dame portrait, and yet the artist has caught something of her. The assured watchful eyes, heavily lidded now and rather menacing; the uneven mouth, firm but mobile. It seems to me not a very good picture, but it is a reasonable likeness and tells us something of her. In fact she has become as she appears here—a mixture of herself and her possessions.

On her return to Australia for the last time she set to work refurnishing her house with the things she had brought from England.

Her home was next door to that of my parents. She still possessed considerable nervous energy but lacked the concentration necessary to employ it in a satisfying way. Her investments occupied a good deal of her time. Failing other distractions she would replant her garden or redecorate her house. My grandmother was very absent-minded and, as she could never find the keys of her safe, developed the habit of hiding her pieces of jewellery in all sorts of odd places—under carpets, in vases, down the backs of chairs. Presently she would forget where she had put them and, convinced she had been robbed, send for the insurance people and the police. Finally the missing articles would be found and my father would have to smooth everybody with fair words and the whisky decanter.

Once, having a large crop of apricots, she decided she would herself make some jam, a process of which her ignorance was complete. As with her other undertakings, it was to be on a grand scale. Her chauffeur set up in the garden a sort of giant witch's cauldron and under it lit a large fire. "Hullo," said my father strolling by, "what's this? It looks like a promising *auto da fé*."

"I am making jam," said my grandmother. "Pour in the fruit, Wallace."

The chauffeur poured in baskets of fruit, bags of sugar. My father looked relieved. "I feared it might be the Bishop of Willochra," he said, for the bishop had recently been staying with her.

The fire burned, the cauldron bubbled. A smell of burnt sugar filled the air.

"How are you going to stop it?" asked my father. "When the jam is cooked, I mean."

My grandmother reached a swift decision. "I shall put the fire out. Wallace, get a hose."

But the hose would not reach. After some delay Wallace fetched a fire-extinguisher. "Stand back, my lady," said the resourceful man and pressed the plunger. Quite soon the flames were smothered. The jam now much reminded me of those tubs of boiling pitch which were a feature of roadmaking operations in those days. Moreover, its surface was covered with foam from the extinguisher. But my grandmother, tasting it, pronounced it delicious. My father politely declined a sample.

"I am going to the House," he said, "and hope to make a speech."

It was offered to me.

"Not the children," said my father firmly. My grandmother gave him a look of hate faintly tinged with respect.

"We shall now bottle it," she announced.

My father drifted away.

In due course the end product was delivered to favoured acquaintances, some of whom, despite my father's warnings, were foolish enough to eat it. For, one mouthful and the teeth were clamped together as with cement while the contents of the fire-extinguisher ate rapidly and painfully into the lips and mouth. The distress of the victims was acute. My mother advised her parent not to eat it

herself. She replied, "Certainly not. I shouldn't dream of
it. I never eat jam. Do you take me for a fool, Penelope?"
There was only one answer to that.

My grandmother had very few friends and they were
without exception intelligent and really good people. I
suppose they had to be.

She had known and admired Dame Nellie Melba for
many years but they were too much alike and each cordially
detested and vigorously maligned the other.

With the exception of her chauffeur, Wallace, her employ-
ees seldom stayed long with her. Wallace was a burly, jolly
ex-soldier and he had a wonderful sense of humour. He
liked my grandmother well enough to put up with her and
she, for her part, did not mind his arguing the point or
even laughing at her. They were in fact very good friends.

For the last ten years of her life all her friends and
relatives, except my mother, called her Agda. "Agda" was
the best her very small grandchildren could make of grandmother and, because she was a great favourite with children,
I suppose the name pleased her. In any event she liked it
and directed that she would be called Agda henceforth.
As usual she was obeyed.

She had a large red Daimler car and on most afternoons her chauffeur took her for a drive. I remember
her very well in this car as I frequently accompanied her.
A grown person could comfortably stand up in the rear
compartment and one sat at a considerable elevation and
was able to survey the scene in every direction except that
segment occupied by the chauffeur. To enable the passenger
to talk to the driver, there was a primitive intercommunica-
tion system. At the passenger's end were a set of buttons
and a sort of microphone. Pressure on the first button
produced a siren-like shriek which was conveyed by an
amplifier to about half an inch of the driver's ear and
this, of course, was to attract the indolent brute's attention.

The correct drill was then to release the first button, press the second and speak into the microphone, as the telephone manual has it, "in a normal speaking voice". My grandmother did not have a normal speaking voice, it was sharp and commanding in the extreme. Neither did she ever quite distinguish one button from another. As experience taught her the limitations of this wretched device, she used it with increasing ferocity. Her usual method was to press both buttons simultaneously and start shouting. The effect on the unhappy driver was literally convulsive. Neither was this all. Having failed to convey her simple directions by modern methods, she would then revert to more direct means. I would be told to wind down the window and my grandmother would jab him sharply in the back of his neck with her umbrella. He would be rebuked for his inattention, and, her instructions finally made clear, the window would be wound up and she would sit back with that satisfaction one feels on the accomplishment of a tricky, laborious task.

She died suddenly in her Melbourne house after a short illness on 28th May, 1929. Until the last few weeks of her life she had enjoyed unvarying good health. The impact of her personality on her few close friends and relatives had been very strong indeed, and I think it no exaggeration to say that after her death life seemed curiously less exciting.

She had always demanded the centre of the stage and nothing less would have satisfied her. Better to die there than fade out quietly in the wings.

H. B. GULLETT

BUSH STUDIES

A Dreamer

A SWIRL of wet leaves from the night-hidden trees decorating the little station beat against the closed doors of the carriages. The porter hurried along holding his blear-eyed lantern to the different windows, and calling the name of the township in language peculiar to porters. There was only one ticket to collect.

Passengers from far up-country towns have importance from their rarity. He turned his lantern full on this one, as he took her ticket. She looked at him too, and listened to the sound of his voice, as he spoke to the guard. Once she had known every hand at the station. The porter knew everyone in the district. This traveller was a stranger to him.

If her letter had been received, someone would have been waiting with a buggy. She passed through the station. She saw nothing but an ownerless dog, huddled, wet and shivering, in a corner. More for sound she turned to look up the straggling street of the township. Among the she-oaks, bordering the river she knew so well, the wind made ghostly music, unheeded by the sleeping town. There was no other sound, and she turned to the dog with a feeling of kinship. But perhaps the porter had a message! She went back to the platform. He was locking the office door, but paused as though expecting her to speak.

"Wet night!" he said at length, breaking the silence.

Her question resolved itself into a request for the time, though this she already knew. She hastily left him.

She drew her cloak tightly round her. The wind made her umbrella useless for shelter. Wind and rain and darkness lay before her on the walk of three bush miles to her mother's home. Still it was the home of her girlhood, and she knew every inch of the way.

As she passed along the sleeping street, she saw no sign of life till near the end. A light burned in a small shop, and the sound of swift tapping came to her. They work late tonight, she thought, and, remembering their gruesome task, hesitated, half-minded to ask these night workers, for whom they laboured. Was it someone she had known? The long dark walk—she could not—and hastened to lose the sound.

The zigzag course of the railway brought the train again near to her, and this wayfarer stood and watched it tunnelling in the teeth of the wind. Whoof! whoof! its steaming breath hissed at her. She saw the rain spitting viciously at its red mouth. Its speed, as it passed, made her realize the tedious difficulties of her journey, and she quickened her pace. There was the silent tenseness that precedes a storm. From the branch of a tree overhead she heard a watchful mother-bird's warning call, and the twitter of the disturbed nestlings. The tender care of this bird-mother awoke memories of her childhood. What mattered the lonely darkness, when it led to mother. Her forebodings fled, and she faced the old track unheedingly, and ever and ever she smiled, as she foretasted their meeting.

"Daughter!"

"Mother!"

She could feel loving arms around her, and a mother's

sacred kisses. She thrilled, and in her impatience ran, but the wind was angry and took her breath. Then the child near her heart stirred for the first time. The instincts of motherhood awakened in her. Her elated body quivered, she fell on her knees, lifted her hands, and turned her face to God. A vivid flash of lightning flamed above her head. It dulled her rapture. The lightning was very near.

She went on, then paused. Was she on the right track? Back, near the bird's nest, were two roads. One led to home, the other was the old bullock-dray road that the railway had almost usurped. When she should have been careful in her choice, she had been absorbed. It was a long way back to the cross-roads, and she dug in her mind for landmarks. Foremost she recalled the "Bendy Tree", then the "Sisters", whose entwined arms talked, when the wind was from the south. The apple-trees on the creek—split flat, where the cows and calves were always to be found. The wrong track, being nearer the river, had clumps of sheoaks and groups of pines in places. An angled line of lightning illuminated everything, but the violence of the thunder distracted her.

She stood in uncertainty, near-sighted, with all the horror of the unknown that this infirmity could bring. Irresolute, she waited for another flash. It served to convince her she was wrong. Through the bush she turned.

The sky seemed to crack with the lightning; the thunder's suddenness shook her. Among some tall pines she stood awed, while the storm raged.

Then again that indefinite fear struck at her. Restlessly she pushed on till she stumbled, and, with hands outstretched, met some object that moved beneath them as she fell. The lightning showed a group of terrified cattle. Tripping and falling, she ran, she knew not where, but keeping her eyes turned towards the cattle. Aimlessly she pushed on, and unconsciously retraced her steps.

She struck the track she was on when her first doubt
came. If this were the right way, the wheel-ruts would
show. She groped, but the rain had levelled them. There
was nothing to guide her. Suddenly she remembered that
the little clump of pines, where the cattle were, lay between
the two roads. She had gathered mistletoe berries there in
the old days.

She believed, she hoped, she prayed, that she was right.
If so, a little further on, she would come to the "Bendy
Tree". There long ago a runaway horse had crushed its
drunken rider against the bent, distorted trunk. She could
recall how in her young years that tree had ever after had
a weird fascination for her.

She saw its crooked body in the lightning's glare. She
was on the right track, yet dreaded to go on. Her childhood's fear came back. In a transient flash she thought
she saw a horseman galloping furiously towards her. She
placed both her hands protectingly over her heart, and
waited. In the dark interval, above the shriek of the wind, she
thought she heard a cry, then crash came the thunder,
drowning her call of warning. In the next flash she saw
nothing but the tree. "Oh, God, protect me!" she prayed,
and diverging, with a shrinking heart passed on.

The road dipped to the creek. Louder and louder came
the roar of its flooded waters. Even little Dog-trap Gully
was proudly foaming itself hoarse. It emptied below where
she must cross. But there were others that swelled it above.

The noise of the rushing creek was borne to her by the
wind, still fierce, though the rain had lessened. Perhaps
there would be someone to meet her at the bank! Last
time she had come, the night had been fine, and though
she had been met at the station by a neighbour's son, mother
had come to the creek with a lantern and waited for her.
She looked eagerly, but there was no light.

The creek was a banker, but the track led to a plank,

which, lashed to the willows on either bank, was usually above flood-level. A churning sound showed that the water was over the plank, and she must wade along it. She turned to the sullen sky. There was no gleam of light save in her resolute, white face.

Her mouth grew tender, as she thought of the husband she loved, and of their child. Must she dare! She thought of the grey-haired mother, who was waiting on the other side. This dwarfed every tie that had parted them. There was atonement in these difficulties and dangers.

Again her face turned heavenward! "Bless, pardon, protect and guide, strengthen and comfort!" Her mother's prayer.

Steadying herself by the long willow branches, ankle-deep she began. With every step the water deepened.

Malignantly the wind fought her, driving her back, or snapping the brittle stems from her skinned hands. The water was knee-deep now, and every step more hazardous.

She held with her teeth to a thin limb, while she unfastened her hat and gave it to the greedy wind. From the cloak, a greater danger, she could not in her haste free herself; her numbed fingers had lost their cunning.

Soon the water would be deeper, and the support from the branches less secure. Even if they did reach across, she could not hope for much support from their wind-driven, fragile ends.

Still she would not go back. Though the roar of that rushing water was making her giddy, though the deafening wind fought her for every inch, she would not turn back.

Long ago she should have come to her old mother, and her heart gave a bound of savage rapture in thus giving the sweat of her body for the sin of her soul.

Midway the current strengthened. Perhaps if she, deprived of the willows, were swept down, her clothes would keep her afloat. She took firm hold and drew a deep breath to call her child-cry, "Mother!"

The water was deeper and swifter, and from the sparsity of the branches she knew she was nearing the middle. The wind unopposed by the willows was more powerful. Strain as she would, she could reach only the tips of the opposite trees, not hold them.

Despair shook her. With one hand she gripped those that had served her so far, and cautiously drew as many as she could grasp with the other. The wind savagely snapped them, and they lashed her unprotected face. Round and round her bare neck they coiled their stripped fingers. Her mother had planted these willows, and she herself had watched them grow. How could they be so hostile to her!

The creek deepened with every moment she waited. But more dreadful than the giddying water was the distracting noise of the mighty wind, nurtured by the hollows.

The frail twigs of the opposite tree snapped again and again in her hands. She must release her hold of those behind her. If she could make two steps independently, the thicker branches would then be her stay.

"Will you?" yelled the wind. A sudden gust caught her, and, hurling her backwards, swept her down the stream with her cloak for a sail.

She battled instinctively, and her first thought was of the letter-kiss she had left for the husband she loved. Was it to be his last?

She clutched a floating branch, and was swept down with it. Vainly she fought for either bank. She opened her lips to call. The wind made a funnel of her mouth and throat, and a wave of muddy water choked her cry. She struggled desperately, but after a few mouthfuls she ceased. The weird cry from the "Bendy Tree" pierced and conquered the deep-throated wind. Then a sweet dream-voice whispered "Little woman!"

Soft, strong arms carried her on. Weakness aroused the
melting idea that all had been a mistake, and she had been
fighting with friends. The wind even crooned a lullaby.
Above the angry waters her face rose untroubled.

A giant tree's fallen body said, "Thus far!" and in vain
the athletic furious water rushed and strove to throw her
over the barrier. Driven back, it tried to take her with it.
But a jagged arm of the tree snagged her cloak and held
her.

Bruised and half-conscious she was left to her deliverer,
and the back-broken water crept tamed under its old foe.
The hammer of hope awoke her heart. Along the friendly
back of the tree she crawled, and among its bared roots
rested. But it was only to get her breath, for this was mother's
side.

She breasted the rise. Then every horror was of the past
and forgotten, for there in the hollow was home.

And there was the light shining its welcome to her.

She quickened her pace, but did not run—motherhood
is instinct in woman. The rain had come again, and the
wind buffeted her. To breathe was a battle, yet she went
on swiftly, for at the sight of the light her nameless fear
had left her.

She would tell mother how she had heard her call in
the night, and mother would smile her grave smile and
stroke her wet hair, call her "Little woman! My little
woman!" and tell her she had been dreaming, just dreaming. Ah, but mother herself was a dreamer!

The gate was swollen with rain and difficult to open.
It had been opened by mother last time. But plainly her
letter had not reached home. Perhaps the bad weather had
delayed the mail-boy.

There was the light. She was not daunted when the
bark of the old dog brought no one to the door. It might
not be heard inside, for there was such a torrent of water

falling somewhere close. Mechanically her mind located it.
The tank near the house, fed by the spouts, was running
over, cutting channels through the flower beds, and flooding
the paths. Why had not mother diverted the spout to the
other tank!

Something indefinite held her. Her mind went back to
the many times long ago when she had kept alive the light
while mother fixed the spout to save the water that the
dry summer months made precious. It was not like mother,
for such carelessness meant carrying from the creek.

Suddenly she grew cold and her heart trembled. After
she had seen mother, she would come out and fix it, but
just now she could not wait.

She tapped gently, and called, "Mother!"

While she waited she tried to make friends with the
dog. Her heart smote her, in that there had been so long
an interval since she saw her old home that the dog had
forgotten her voice.

Her teeth chattered as she again tapped softly. The sudden
light dazzled her when a stranger opened the door for her.
Steadying herself by the wall, with wild eyes she looked
around. Another strange woman stood by the fire, and a
child slept on the couch. The child's mother raised it, and
the other led the now panting creature to the child's bed.
Not a word was spoken, and the movements of these women
were like those who fear to awaken a sleeper.

Something warm was held to her lips, for through it all
she was conscious of everything, even that the numbing
horror in her eyes met answering awe in theirs.

In the light the dog knew her and gave her welcome.
But she had none for him now.

When she rose one of the women lighted a candle. She
noticed how, if the blazing wood cracked, the women
started nervously, how the disturbed child pointed to her
bruised face, and whispered softly to its mother, how she

who lighted the candle did not strike the match but held it to the fire, and how the light-bearer led the way so noiselessly.

She reached her mother's room. Aloft the woman held the candle and turned away her head.

The daughter parted the curtains, and the light fell on the face of the sleeper who would dream no dreams that night.

Squeaker's Mate

THE woman carried the bag with the axe and maul and wedges; the man had the billy and clean tucker-bags; the cross-cut saw linked them. She was taller than the man, and the equability of her body, contrasting with his indolent slouch, accentuated the difference. "Squeaker's mate", the men called her, and these agreed that she was the best long-haired mate that ever stepped in petticoats. The selectors' wives pretended to challenge her right to womanly garments, but if she knew what they said, it neither turned nor troubled Squeaker's mate.

Nine prospective posts and maybe sixteen rails—she calculated this yellow gum would yield. "Come on," she encouraged the man; "let's tackle it."

From the bag she took the axe, and ring-barked a preparatory circle, while he looked for a shady spot for the billy and tucker-bags.

"Come on." She was waiting with the greased saw. He came. The saw rasped through a few inches, then he stopped and looked at the sun.

"It's nigh tucker-time," he said, and when she dissented, he exclaimed, with sudden energy, "There's another bee! Wait, you go on with the axe, an' I'll track 'im."

As they came, they had already followed one and located

the nest. She could not see the bee he spoke of, though her grey eyes were as keen as a black's. However, she knew the man, and her tolerance was of the mysteries.

She drew out the saw, spat on her hands, and with the axe began weakening the inclining side of the tree.

Long and steadily and in secret the worm had been busy in the heart. Suddenly the axe blade sank softly, the tree's wounded edges closed on it like a vice. There was a "settling" quiver on its top branches, which the woman heard and understood. The man, encouraged by the sounds of the axe, had returned with an armful of sticks for the billy. He shouted gleefully, "It's fallin', look out."

But she waited to free the axe.

With a shivering groan the tree fell, and as she sprang aside, a thick worm-eaten branch snapped at a joint and silently she went down under it.

"I tole yer t' look out," he reminded her, as with a crowbar, and grunting earnestly, he forced it up. "Now get out quick."

She tried moving her arms and the upper part of her body. Do this; do that, he directed, but she made no movement after the first.

He was impatient, because for once he had actually to use his strength. His share of a heavy lift usually consisted of a make-believe grunt, delivered at a critical moment. Yet he hardly cared to let it again fall on her, though he told her he would, if she "didn't shift".

Near him lay a piece broken short; with his foot he drew it nearer, then gradually worked it into a position, till it acted as a stay to the lever.

He laid her on her back when he drew her out, and waited expecting some acknowledgment of his exertions, but she was silent, and as she did not notice that the axe, she had tried to save, lay with the fallen trunk across it, he told her. She cared almost tenderly for all their posessions and treated them as friends. But the half-buried broken axe did not affect her. He wondered a little, for only last week she had patiently chipped out the old broken head, and put in a new handle.

"Feel bad?" he inquired at length.

"Pipe," she replied with slack lips.

Both pipes lay in the fork of a near tree. He took his, shook out the ashes, filled it, picked up a coal and puffed till it was alight—then he filled hers. Taking a small fire-stick he handed her the pipe. The hand she raised shook and closed in an uncertain hold, but she managed by a great effort to get it to her mouth. He lost patience with the swaying hand that tried to take the light.

"Quick," he said "quick, that damn dog's at the tucker."

He thrust it into her hand that dropped helplessly across her chest. The lighted stick, falling between her bare arm and the dress, slowly roasted the flesh and smouldered the clothes.

He rescued their dinner, pelted his dog out of sight—hers was lying near her head—put on the billy, then came back to her.

The pipe had fallen from her lips; there was blood on the stem.

"Did yer jam yer tongue?" he asked.

She always ignored trifles, he knew, therefore he passed her silence.

He told her that her dress was on fire. She took no heed. He put it out, and looked at the burnt arm, then with intentness at her.

Her eyes were turned unblinkingly to the heavens, her lips were grimly apart, and a strange greyness was upon her face, and the sweat-beads were mixing.

"Like a drink er tea? Asleep?"

He broke a green branch from the fallen tree and swished

from his face the multitudes of flies that had descended with it.

In a heavy way he wondered why did she sweat, when she was not working? Why did she not keep the flies out of her mouth and eyes? She'd have bungy eyes, if she didn't. If she was asleep, why did she not close them?

But asleep or awake, as the billy began to boil, he left her, made the tea, and ate his dinner. His dog had disappeared, and as it did not come to his whistle, he threw the pieces to hers, that would not leave her head to reach them.

He whistled tunelessly his one air, beating his own time with a stick on the toe of his blucher, then looked overhead at the sun and calculated that she must have been lying like that for "close up an hour". He noticed that the axe handle was broken in two places, and speculated a little as to whether she would again pick out the back-broken handle or burn it out in his method, which was less trouble, if it did spoil the temper of the blade. He examined the worm-dust in the stump and limbs of the newly-fallen tree; mounted it and looked round the plain. The sheep were straggling in a manner that meant walking work to round them, and he supposed he would have to yard them tonight, if she didn't liven up. He looked down at unenlivened her. This changed his "chune" to a call for his hiding dog.

"Come on, ole feller," he commanded her dog. "Fetch 'em back." He whistled further instructions, slapping his thigh and pointing to the sheep.

But a brace of wrinkles either side the brute's closed mouth demonstrated determined disobedience. The dog would go if she told him, and by and by she would.

He lighted his pipe and killed half an hour smoking. With the frugality that hard graft begets, his mate limited both his and her own tobacco, so he must not smoke all afternoon. There was no work to shirk, so time began to drag. Then a "goanner" crawling up a tree attracted him.

He gathered various missiles and tried vainly to hit the
seemingly grinning reptile. He came back and sneaked a
fill of her tobacco, and while he was smoking, the white
tilt of a cart caught his eye. He jumped up. "There's Red
Bob goin' t'our place fur th' 'oney," he said. "I'll go an'
weigh it an' get the gonz" (money).

He ran for the cart, and kept looking back as if fearing
she would follow and thwart him.

Red Bob the dealer was, in a business way, greatly concerned, when he found that Squeaker's mate was " 'avin' a
sleep out there 'cos a tree fell on her". She was the best
honey-strainer and boiler that he dealt with. She was straight
and square too. There was no water in her honey whether
boiled or merely strained, and in every kerosene-tin the
weight of honey was to an ounce as she said. Besides he
was suspicious and diffident of paying the indecently eager
Squeaker before he saw the woman. So reluctantly Squeaker
led to where she lay. With many fierce oaths Red Bob
sent her lawful protector for help, and compassionately
poured a little from his flask down her throat, then swished
away the flies from her till help came.

Together these men stripped a sheet of bark, and laying
her with pathetic tenderness upon it, carried her to her hut.
Squeaker followed in the rear with the billy and tucker.

Red Bob took his horse from the cart, and went to town
for the doctor. Late that night at the back of the old hut
(there were two) he and others who had heard that she
was hurt, squatted with unlighted pipes in their mouths,
waiting to hear the doctor's verdict. After he had given
it and gone, they discussed in whispers, and with a look seen
only on bush faces, the hard luck of that woman who alone
had hard-grafted with the best of them for every acre and
hoof on that selection. Squeaker would go through it in no
time. Why she had allowed it to be taken up in his name,

when the money had been her own, was also for them among the mysteries.

Him they called "a nole woman", not because he was hanging round the honey-tins, but after man's fashion to eliminate all virtue. They beckoned him, and explaining his mate's injury, cautioned him to keep from her the knowledge that she would be for ever a cripple.

"Jus' th' same, now, then fur 'im," pointing to Red Bob, "t' pay me, I'll 'ev t' go t' town."

They told him in whispers what they thought of him, and with a cowardly look towards where she lay, but without a word of parting, like shadows these men made for their homes.

Next day the women came. Squeaker's mate was not a favourite with them—a woman with no leisure for yarning was not likely to be. After the first day they left her severely alone, their plea to their husbands, her uncompromising independence. It is in the ordering of things that by degrees most husbands accept their wives' views of other women.

The flour bespattering Squeaker's now neglected clothes spoke eloquently of his clumsy efforts at damper making. The women gave him many a feed, agreeing that it must be miserable for him.

If it were miserable and lonely for his mate, she did not complain; for her the long, long days would give place to longer nights—those nights with the pregnant bush silence suddenly cleft by a bush voice. However, she was not fanciful, and being a bush scholar knew 'twas a dingo, when a long whine came from the scrub on the skirts of which lay the axe under the worm-eaten tree. That quivering wail from the billabong lying murkily mystic towards the East was only the cry of the fearing curlew.

Always her dog—wakeful and watchful as she—patiently

waiting for her to be up and about again. That would be soon, she told her complaining mate.

"Yer won't. Yer back's broke," said Squeaker laconically. "That's wot's wrong er yer; injoory t' th' spine. Doctor says that means back's broke, and yer won't never walk no more. No good not t' tell yer, cos I can't be doin' everythin'."

A wild look grew on her face, and she tried to sit up.

"Erh," said he, "see! yer carnt, yer jes' ther same as a snake w'en ees back's broke, on'y yer don't bite yerself like a snake does w'en 'e carnt crawl. Yer did bite yer tongue w'en yer fell."

She gasped, and he could hear her heart beating when she let her head fall back a few moments; though she wiped her wet forehead with the back of her hand, and still said that was the doctor's mistake. But day after day she tested her strength, and whatever the result, was silent, though white witnesses, halo-wise, gradually circled her brow and temples.

"'Tisn't as if yer was agoin' t' get better t'morrer, the doctor says yer won't never work no more, an' I can't be cookin' an' workin' an' doin' everythin'!"

He muttered something about "sellin' out", but she firmly refused to think of such a monstrous proposal.

He went into town one Saturday afternoon soon after, and did not return till Monday.

Her supplies, a billy of tea and scraps of salt beef and damper (her dog got the beef), gave out the first day, though that was as nothing to her compared with the bleat of the penned sheep, for it was summer and droughty, and her dog could not unpen them.

Of them and her dog only she spoke when he returned. He d—d him, and d—d her, and told her to "double up yer ole broke back an' bite yerself". He threw things about, made a long-range feint of kicking her threatening dog, then sat outside in the shade of the old hut, nursing his head till he slept.

She, for many reasons, had when necessary made these trips into town, walking both ways, leading a pack-horse for supplies. She never failed to indulge him in a half pint—a pipe was her luxury.

The sheep waited till next day, so did she.

For a few days he worked a little in her sight; not much —he never did. It was she who always lifted the heavy end of the log, and carried the tools; he—the billy and tucker.

She wearily watched him idling his time; reminded him that the wire lying near the fence would rust, one could run the wire through easily, and when she got up in a day or so, she would help strain and fasten it. At first he pretended he had done it, later said he wasn't goin' t' go wirin' or nothin' else by 'imself if every other man on the place did.

She spoke of many other things that could be done by one, reserving the great till she was well. Sometimes he whistled while she spoke, often swore, generally went out, and when this was inconvenient, dull as he was, he found the "Go and bite yerself like a snake", would instantly silence her.

At last the work worry ceased to exercise her, and for night to bring him home was a rare thing.

Her dog rounded and yarded the sheep when the sun went down and there was no sign of him, and together they kept watch on their movements till dawn. She was mindful not to speak of this care to him, knowing he would have left it for them to do constantly, and she noticed that what little interest he seemed to share went to the sheep. Why, was soon demonstrated.

Through the cracks her ever watchful eyes one day saw the dust rise out of the plain. Nearer it came till she saw

him and a man on horseback rounding and driving the
sheep into the yard, and later both left in charge of a little
mob. Their "Baa-baas" to her were cries for help; many
had been pets. So he was selling her sheep to the town
butchers.

In the middle of the next week he came from town with
a fresh horse, new saddle and bridle. He wore a flash red
shirt, and round his neck a silk handkerchief. On the next
occasion she smelt scent, and though he did not try to
display the dandy meerschaum, she saw it, and heard the
squeak of the new boots, not bluchers. However he was
kinder to her this time, offering a fill of his cut tobacco;
he had long ceased to keep her supplied. Several of the
men who sometimes in passing took a look in, would have
made up her loss had they known, but no word of com-
plaint passed her lips.

She looked at Squeaker as he filled his pipe from his
pouch, but he would not meet her eyes, and, seemingly
dreading something, slipped out.

She heard him hammering in the old hut at the back,
which served for tools and other things which sunlight
and rain did not hurt. Quite briskly he went in and out.
She could see him through the cracks carrying a narrow
strip of bark, and understood, he was making a bunk.
When it was finished he had a smoke, then came to her
and fidgetted about; he said this hut was too cold, and that
she would never get well in it. She did not feel cold, but,
submitting to his mood, allowed him to make a fire that
would roast a sheep. He took off his hat, and, fanning himself, said he was roastin', wasn't she? She was.

He offered to carry her into the other; he would put
a new roof on it in a day or two, and it would be better
than this one, and she would be up in no time. He stood
to say this where she could not see him.

His eagerness had tripped him.

There were months to run before all the Government conditions of residence, etc., in connection with the selection, would be fulfilled, still she thought perhaps he was trying to sell out, and she would not go.

He was away four days that time, and when he returned slept in the new bunk.

She compromised. Would he put a bunk there for himself, keep out of town, and not sell the place? He promised instantly with additions.

"Try could yer crawl yerself?" he coaxed, looking at her bulk.

Her nostrils quivered with her suppressed breathing, and her lips tightened, but she did not attempt to move.

It was evident some great purpose actuated him. After attempts to carry and drag her, he rolled her on the sheet of bark that had brought her home, and laboriously drew her round.

She asked for a drink, he placed her billy and tin pint besides the bunk, and left her, gasping and dazed, to her sympathetic dog.

She saw him run up and yard his horse, and though she called him, he would not answer nor come.

When he rode swiftly towards the town, her dog leaped on the bunk, and joined a refrain to her lamentation, but the cat took to the bush.

He came back at dusk next day in a spring cart—not alone—he had another mate. She saw her though he came a roundabout way, trying to keep in front of the new hut.

There were noises of moving many things from the cart to the hut. Finally he came to a crack near where she lay, and whispered the promise of many good things to her if she kept quiet, and that he would set her hut afire if she didn't. She was quiet, he need not have feared, for that time she was past it, she was stunned.

The released horse came stumbling round to the old hut, and thrust its head in the door in a domesticated fashion. Her dog promptly resented this straggler mistaking their hut for a stable. And the dog's angry dissent, together with the shod clatter of the rapidly disappearing intruder, seemed to have a disturbing effect on the pair in the new hut. The settling sounds suddenly ceased, and the cripple heard the stranger close the door, despite Squeaker's assurances that the woman in the old hut could not move from her bunk to save her life, and that her dog would not leave her.

Food, more and better, was placed near her—but, dumb and motionless, she lay with her face turned to the wall, and her dog growled menacingly at the stranger. The new woman was uneasy, and told Squeaker what people might say and do if she died.

He scared at the "do", went into the bush and waited.

She went to the door, not the crack, the face was turned that way, and said she had come to cook and take care of her.

The disabled woman, turning her head slowly, looked steadily at her. She was not much to look at. Her red hair hung in an uncurled bang over her forehead, the lower part of her face had robbed the upper, and her figure evinced imminent motherhood, though it is doubtful if the barren woman, noting this, knew by calculation the paternity was not Squeaker's. She was not learned in these matters, though she understood all about an ewe and lamb.

One circumstance was apparent—ah! bitterest of all bitterness to women—she was younger.

The thick hair that fell from the brow of the woman on the bunk was white now.

Bread and butter the woman brought. The cripple looked at it, at her dog, at the woman. Bread and butter for a dog! but the stranger did not understand till she saw it offered to the dog. The bread and butter was not for the dog. She brought meat.

All next day the man kept hidden. The cripple saw his dog, and knew he was about.

But there was an end of this pretence when at dusk he came back with a show of haste, and a finger of his right hand bound and ostentatiously prominent. His entrance caused great excitement to his new mate. The old mate, who knew this snake-bite trick from its inception, maybe, realized how useless were the terrified stranger's efforts to rouse the snoring man after an empty pint bottle had been flung on the outside heap.

However, what the sick woman thought was not definite, for she kept silent always. Neither was it clear how much she ate, and how much she gave to her dog, though the new mate said to Squeaker one day that she believed that the dog would not take a bite more than its share.

The cripple's silence told on the stranger, especially when alone. She would rather have abuse. Eagerly she counted the days past and to pass. Then back to the town. She told no word of that hope to Squeaker, he had no place in her plans for the future. So if he spoke of what they would do by and by when his time would be up, and he able to sell out, she listened in uninterested silence.

She did tell him she was afraid of "her", and after the first day would not go within reach, but every morning made a billy of tea, which with bread and beef Squeaker carried to her.

The rubbish heap was adorned, for the first time, with jam and fish tins from the table in the new hut. It seemed to be understood that neither woman nor dog in the old hut required them.

Squeaker's dog sniffed and barked joyfully around them till his licking efforts to bottom a salmon tin sent him careering in a muzzled frenzy, that caused the younger woman's thick lips to part grinningly till he came too close.

The remaining sheep were regularly yarded. His old mate heard him whistle as he did it. Squeaker began to work about a little burning-off. So that now, added to the other bush voices, was the call from some untimely falling giant. There is no sound so human as that from the riven souls of these tree people, or the trembling sighs of their upright neighbours whose hands in time will meet over the victim's fallen body.

There was no bunk on the side of the hut to which her eyes turned, but her dog filled that space, and the flash that passed between this back-broken woman and her dog might have been the spirit of these slain tree folk, it was so wondrous ghostly. Still, at times, the practical in her would be dominant, for in a mind so free of fancies, backed by bodily strength, hope died slowly, and forgetful of self she would almost call to Squeaker her fears that certain bees' nests were in danger.

He went into town one day and returned, as he had promised, long before sundown, and next day a clothes-line bridged the space between two trees near the back of the old hut; and—an equally rare occurrence—Squeaker placed across his shoulders the yoke that his old mate had fashioned for herself, with two kerosene-tins attached, and brought them filled with water from the distant creek; but both only partly filled the tub, a new purchase. With utter disregard of the heat and Squeaker's sweating brow, his new mate said, even after another trip, two more now for the blue water. Under her commands he brought them, though sullenly, perhaps contrasting the old mate's methods with the new.

His old mate had periodically carried their washing to the creek, and his mole-skins had been as white as snow without aid of blue.

Towards noon, on the clothes-line many strange garments

fluttered, suggestive of a taunt to the barren woman. When the sun went down she could have seen the assiduous Squeaker lower the new prop-sticks and considerately stoop to gather the pegs his inconsiderate new mate had dropped. However, after one load of water next morning, on hearing her estimate that three more would put her own things through, Squeaker struck. Nothing he could urge would induce the stranger to trudge to the creek, where thirst-slaked snakes lay waiting for someone to bite. She sulked and pretended to pack up, till a bright idea struck Squeaker. He fastened a cask on a sledge and, harnessing the new horse, hitched him to it, and, under the approving eyes of his new mate, led off to the creek, though, when she went inside, he bestrode the spiritless brute.

He had various mishaps, any one of which would have served as an excuse to his old mate, but even babes soon know on whom to impose. With an energy new to him he persevered and filled the cask, but the old horse repudiated such a burden even under Squeaker's unmerciful welts. Almost half was sorrowfully baled out, and under a rain of whacks the horse shifted it a few paces, but the cask tilted and the thirsty earth got its contents. All Squeaker's adjectives over his wasted labour were as unavailing as the cure for spilt milk.

It took skill and patience to rig the cask again. He partly filled it, and, just as success seemed probable, the rusty wire fastening the cask to the sledge snapped with the strain, and, springing free, coiled affectionately round the terrified horse's hocks. Despite the sledge (the cask had been soon disposed of) that old town horse's pace then was his record. Hours after, on the plain that met the horizon, loomed two specks: the distance between them might be gauged, for the larger was Squeaker.

Anticipating a plentiful supply and lacking in bush caution, the new mate used the half-bucket of water to boil

the salt mutton. Towards noon she laid this joint and bread
on the rough table, then watched anxiously in the wrong
direction for Squeaker.

She had drained the new tea-pot earlier, but she placed
the spout to her thirsty mouth again.

She continued looking for him for hours.

Had he sneaked off to town, thinking she had not used
that water, or not caring whether or no? She did not trust
him; another had left her. Besides she judged Squeaker
by his treatment of the woman who was lying in there with
wide-open eyes. Anyhow no use to cry with only that silent
woman to hear her.

Had she drunk all hers?

She tried to see at long range through the cracks, but
the hanging bed-clothes hid the billy, She went to the
door, and, avoiding the bunk looked at the billy.

It was half full.

Instinctively she knew that the eyes of the woman were
upon her. She turned away, and hoped and waited for
thirsty minutes that seemed hours.

Desperation drove her back to the door. Dared she? No,
she couldn't.

Getting a long forked propstick, she tried to reach it from
the door, but the dog sprang at the stick. She dropped it
and ran.

A scraggy growth fringed the edge of the plain. There
was the creek. How far? she wondered. Oh, very far, she
knew, and besides there were only a few holes where water
was, and the snakes; for Squeaker, with a desire to shine
in her eyes, was continually telling her of snakes—vicious
and many—that daily he did battle with.

She recalled the evening he came from hiding in the
scrub with a string round one finger, and said a snake had
bitten him. He had drunk the pint of brandy she had
brought for her sickness, and then slept till morning. True,

although next day he had to dig for the string round the blue swollen finger, he was not worse than the many she had seen at the Shearer's Rest suffering a recovery. There was no brandy to cure her if she were bitten.

She cried a little in self-pity, then withdrew her eyes, that were getting red, from the outlying creek, and went again to the door. She of the bunk lay with closed eyes.

Was she asleep? The stranger's heart leapt, yet she was hardly in earnest as she tip-toed billy-wards. The dog, crouching with head between two paws, eyed her steadily, but showed no opposition. She made dumb show. "I want to be friends with you, and won't hurt her." Abruptly she looked at her, then at the dog. He was motionless and emotionless. Besides if that dog—certainly watching her— wanted to bite her (her dry mouth opened) it could get her any time.

She rated this dog's intelligence almost human, from many of its actions in omission and commission in connection with this woman.

She regretted the pole, no dog would stand that.

Two more steps.

Now just one more; then, by bending and stretching her arm, she would reach it. Could she now? She tried to encourage herself by remembering how close on the first day she had been to the woman, and how delicious a few mouthfuls would be—swallowing dry mouthfuls.

She measured the space between where she had first stood and the billy. Could she get anything to draw it to her? No, the dog would not stand that, and besides the handle would rattle, and she might hear and open her eyes.

The thought of those sunken eyes suddenly opening made her heart bound. Oh! she must breathe—deep, loud breaths. Her throat clicked noisily. Looking back fearfully, she went swiftly out.

She did not look for Squeaker this time, she had given him up.

While she waited for her breath to steady, to her relief and surprise the dog came out. She made a rush to the new hut, but he passed seemingly oblivious of her, and, bounding across the plain, began rounding the sheep. Then he must know Squeaker had gone to town.

Stay! Her heart beat violently; was it because she on the bunk slept and did not want him?

She waited till her heart quieted, and again crept to the door.

The head of the woman on the bunk had fallen towards the wall as in deep sleep; it was turned from the billy, to which she must creep so softly.

Slower, from caution and deadly earnestness, she entered.

She was not so advanced as before, and felt fairly secure, for the woman's eyes were still turned to the wall, and so tightly closed she could not possibly see where she was.

She would bend right down, and try and reach it from where she was.

She bent.

It was so swift and sudden, that she had not time to scream when those bony fingers had gripped the hand that she prematurely reached for the billy. She was frozen with horror for a moment, then her screams were piercing. Panting with victory, the prostrate one held her with a hold that the other did not attempt to free herself from.

Down, down she drew her.

Her lips had drawn back from her teeth, and her breath almost scorched the face that she held so close for the staring eyes to gloat over. Her exultation was so great that she could only gloat and gasp, and hold with a tension that had stopped the victim's circulation.

As a wounded, robbed tigress might hold and look, she held and looked.

Neither heard the swift steps of the man, and if the tigress saw him enter, she was not daunted. "Take me from her," shrieked the terrified one. "Quick, take me from her," she repeated it again, nothing else. "Take me from her."

He hastily fastened the door and said something that the shrieks drowned, then picked up the pole. It fell with a thud across the arms which the tightening sinews had turned into steel. Once, twice, thrice. Then the one that got the fullest force bent; that side of the victim was free.

The pole had snapped. Another blow with a broken end freed the other side.

Still shrieking "Take me from her, take me from her, she beat on the closed door till Squeaker opened it.

Then he had to face and reckon with his old mate's maddened dog, that the closed door had baffled.

The dog suffered the shrieking woman to pass, but though Squeaker, in bitten agony, broke the stick across the dog, he was forced to give the savage brute best.

"Call 'im orf, Mary, 'e's eatin' me," he implored. "Oh corl 'im orf."

But with stony face the woman lay motionless.

"Sool 'im on t' 'er." He indicated his new mate who, as though all the plain led to the desired town, still ran in unreasoning terror.

"It's orl er doin'," he pleaded, springing on the bunk beside his old mate. But when, to rouse her sympathy, he would have laid his hand on her, the dog's teeth fastened in it and pulled him back.

Scrammy 'And

ALONG the selvage of the scrub-girt plain the old man looked long and earnestly. His eyes followed an indistinct track that had been cut by the cart, journeying at rare intervals to the distant township. At dawn some weeks back it had creaked across the plain, and at a point where the scrub curved, the husband had stopped the horse while the woman parted the tilt and waved goodbye to the bent, irresponsive old man and his dog. It was her impending motherhood that made them seek the comparative civilization of the township, and the tenderness of her womanhood brought the old man closer to her as they drove away. Every week since that morning had been carefully notched by man and dog, and the last mark, cut three nights past, showed that time was up. Twice this evening he thought he saw the dust rise as he looked, but longer scrutiny showed only the misty evening light.

He turned to where a house stood out from a background of scrub. Beside the calf-pen near it, a cow gave answer and greeting to the penned calf. "No use pennin' up ther calf," he muttered, "when they don't come. Won't do it termorrer night." He watched anxiously along the scrub. "Calf must 'ave got 'is 'ed through ther rails an' sucked 'er. No one else can't 'ave done it. Scrammy's gorn;

'twarn't Scrammy." But the gloom of fear settled on his wizened face as he shuffled stiffly towards the sheepyard.

His body jerked; there was a suggestion of the dog in his movements; and in the dog, as he rounded up the sheep, more than a suggestion of his master. He querulously accused the dog of "rushin' 'em, 'stead er allowin' Billy" (the leader) "to lead 'em".

When they were yarded he found fault with the hurdles. "Some un 'ad been meddlin' with 'em." For two pins he would "smash 'em up with ther axe".

The eyes of the sheep reflected the haze-opposed glory of the setting sun. Loyally they stood till a grey quilt swathed them. In their eyes glistened luminous tears materialized from an atmosphere of sighs. The wide plain gauzed into a sea on which the hut floated lonely. Through its open door a fire gleamed like the red, steaming mouth of an engine. Beyond the hut a clump of myalls loomed spectral and wraith-like, and round them a gang of crows cawed noisily, irreverent of the great silence.

Inside the hut, the old man, still querulous, talked to the listening dog. He uncovered a cabbage-tree hat—his task of the past year—and laid upside down, on the centre of the crown, a star-shaped button that the woman had worked for him.

"It's orl wrong, see!" The dog said he did. " 'Twon't do!" he shouted with the emphasis of deafness. The dog admitted it would not. "An' she done it like thet, ter spile it on me er purpus. She done it outer jealersy, cos I was makin' it for 'im. Could 'ave done it better meself, though I'm no 'and at fancy stitchin'. But she can't make a 'at like thet. No woman could. The're no good." The dog did not dispute this condemnation.

"I tole 'er ter put a anker jes' there," he continued. He pointed to the middle of the button which he still held upside down. "Thet's no anker!" The dog subtly indicated

that there was another side to the button. "There ain't,"
shouted the old man. "What do you know about an anker;
you never see a real one on a ship in yer life!" There was
an inaudible disparaging reference to "imperdent ker-
loneyals" which seemed to crush the dog. To mollify him
the man got on his knees and, bending his neck, showed
the dog a faded anchor on the top of the cabbage-tree hat
on his head. A little resentment would have served the dog,
but he was too eager for peace.

Noting this, the old man returned to the button for
reminiscences. "An' yet you thort at fust a thing like thet
would do." There was a sign of dissent from the dog. "Yer
know yer did—Sir. An' wot's more yer don't bark at 'er
like yer used ter!"

The dog was uneasy, and intimated that he would prefer
to have that past buried.

"None er thet now; yer know yer don't." Bending the
button he continued, "They can't never do anythin' right,
an' orlways, continerally they gets a man inter trouble."

He had accidentally turned the button, he reversed it
looking swiftly at the dog. "Carn't do nothin' with it. A
thing like thet! Might as well fling it in the fire!" He put it
carefully away.

"W'ere's 'e now?" he asked abruptly. The dog indicated
the route taken by the cart.

"An' 'ow long as 'e bin away?" The dog looked at the
tally stick hanging on the wall. "Yes, orl thet time! What
does 'e care about me an' you, now 'e's got 'er! 'E was fust
rate afore 'e got 'er. Wish I 'ad er gorn down thet time 'e
took their sheep. I'd er seen no woman didn't grab 'im.
They're stuck away down there an' us orl alone 'ere by
ourselves with only ther sheep. Scrammy sez 'e wouldn't
stay if 'e wus me. See's there any signs er 'em comin'
back!"

While the dog was out he hastily tried to fix the button,

but failed. "On'y mist, no dust?" he asked, when his messenger returned. "No fear," he growled, " 'e won't come back no more; stay down there an' nuss ther babby. It'll be a gal too, sure to be! Women are orlways 'avin' gals. It'll be a gal sure enough."

He looked sternly at the unagreeing dog. "Yer don't think so! Course yer don't. You on 'er side? Yer are, Loo!"

The dog's name was "Warderloo" (Waterloo) and had three abbreviations. "Now then, War!" meant mutual understanding and perfect fellowship. "What's thet, Warder?" meant serious business. But "Loo" was ever sorrowfully reminiscent. And accordingly Loo was now much affected and disconcerted by the steady accusing eyes of the old man.

"An' wot's more," he continued, "I believe ye'll fool roun', ye'll fool aroun' 'er wusser nor ever w'en she comes back with ther babby." At this grave charge the dog, either from dignity or injury, was silent. His master, slowly and with some additions, repeated the prophecy, and again the dog gave him only silent attention.

" 'Ere she comes with ther babby," he cried, flinging up his arms in clumsy feigned surprise. Loo was not deceived, and stood still.

"Oh I'm a ole liar, am I! Yit's come ter thet; ez it? Well better fer I ter be a liar 'n fer you ter lose yer manners —Sir."

In vain Loo protested. His master turned round, and when poor Loo faced that way, he drew his feet under him on the bunk and faced the wall. When the distressed Loo, from outside the hut, caught his eye through the cracks, he closed his own, to stifle remorse at the eloquent dumb appeal.

Usually their little differences took some time to evaporate; the master sulked with his silent mate till some daring feat with snake or dingo on the dog's part mollified him.

Loo, probably on the look-out for such foes, moved to the end of the hut nearest the sheep. Two hasty squints revealed his departure, but not his whereabouts, to the old man, who coughed and waited, but for once expected too much from poor Loo. His legs grew cramped, still he did not care to make the first move. It was a godsend when an undemonstrative ewe and demonstrative lamb came in.

Before that ewe he held the whole of her disgraceful past, and under the circumstances, " 'er imperdence—'er blarsted imperdence—" in unceremoniously intruding on his privacy with her blanky blind udder, and more than blanky bastard, was something he could not and would not stand.

"None er yer sauce, now!" He jumped down, and shook his fist at the unashamed, silent mother. "Warder," he shouted, "Warder, put 'em out!"

Warder did so, and when he came back his master explained to him that the thing that "continerally an' orlways" upset him was "thet dam old yoe". It was the only sorrow he had or ever would have in life. "She wusn't nat'ral, thet ole yoe." There was something in the Bible, he told War, about "yoes" with barren udders. "An' 'twarn't as though she didn't know." For that was her third lamb he had had to poddy. But not another bite would he give this one. He had made up his mind now, though it had been worritin' him all day. "Jes' look at me," showing his lamb-bitten fingers. "Wantin' ter get blood outer a stone!"

He shambled round, covered the cabbage-tree hat and the despised woman-worked button carefully; then his better nature prevailed. "See 'ere!" and there was that in his voice that indicated a moral victory. He took off the cloth and placed the button right side up and in its proper place. "Will thet do yer?" he asked.

After this surrender his excitement was so great that the dog shared it. He advised War to lie down "an' 'ave a

spell", and in strong agitation he went round the sheepyard twice, each time stopping to hammer down the hurdles
noisily, and calling to War not to "worrit; they's orlright
now, an' firm as a rock."

Through these proceedings the ewe and lamb followed
him, the lamb—lamb fashion—mixing itself with his legs.
He had nothing further to say to the ewe, but from the
expression of her eyes she still had an open mind towards
him. Both went with him inside the hut. Were they
intruders? the dog asked. He coughed and affected not to
hear, went to the door, looked out and said the mist was
gone, but the dog re-asked. "I think, War, there's some er
that orker'd little dam' fool's grub lef'," he said, gently
extricating the lamb from between his legs, "an' it'll on'y
spile. Jes' this once 'an no more, min' yer, an' then you
skiddy addy," he said to the ewe. He carried the lamb outside, for he would not finger-suckle it that night before
Waterloo.

From his bunk-head he took an axe, cut in two a myall
log, and brought in half. He threw it on the fire for a
back-log, first scraping the live coals and ashes to a heap
for his damper.

He filled and trimmed his slush-lamp, and from a series
of flat pockets hanging on the wall he took thread, needle,
and beeswax. He hung a white cloth in a way that defined
the eye of the needle which he held at long range; but
vary as he would from long to longest the thread remained
in one hand, the needle in the other. Needle, thread, light,
everything was wrong, he told War. "Es fer me, thenk a
Lord I ken see an' year's well's ever I could. Ehm, War!
See any change?" War said there had been no change
observable to him. "There ain't no change in you neither,
War!" he said in gratitude to the grizzled old dog. But he
felt that War had been disappointed at his failure, and he

promised that he would rise betimes tomorrow and sew on the button by daylight.

"Never mind, War; like ter see 'em after supper?" Comradeship was never by speech better demonstrated.

From the middle beam the old man untied two bags. Boiled mutton was in one, and the heel of a damper in another.

"No blowey carn't get in there, eh?" the dog looked at the meat uncritically, but critically noted the resting place of two disturbed "bloweys".

"No bones!" He had taken great care to omit them. "Neow!" As ever, War took his word; he caught and swallowed instantly several pieces flung to him. At the finish his master's "Eny?" referred to bones. War's grateful eyes twinkled, "Not a one." "Never is neow!" had reference to a trouble War had had with one long ago.

It was now time for his own supper, but after a few attempts he shirked it. "Blest if I evven fergot t'bile th' billy; funny ef me t' ferget!" He held his head for a moment, then filled the billy, and in a strange uncertainty went towards and from the fire with it, and in the end War thought there was no sense at all in putting it so far from the blaze when it had to boil.

"Tell yer wot, War, w'ile it biles us'll count 'em. Gimme appertite, ehm, War?"

War thought "countin' 'em" was the tonic. Then together they closed the door, spread a kangaroo-skin on the floor, and put the slush-lamp where the light fell on it. The man sat down, so did War, took off his belt, turned it carefully, tenderly, and opened his knife to cut the stitching. This was a tedious process, for it was wax thread, and had been crossed and recrossed. Then came the chink of the coins falling. The old man counted each as it rolled out, and the dog tallied with a paw.

"No more?" Certainly more, said War. A jerk, tenderly calculated, brought another among the seductive heap.

"All?" no—still the upraised paw. The old man chuckled. "Ole 'en gets more b' scratchin'." This was the dog's opinion, and a series of little undulations produced another, and after still further shaking, yet another.

War was asked with ridiculous insincerity, "All?" and with ridiculous sincerity his solemn eyes and dropped paw said "All". Then there was the honest count straight through, next the side show with its pretence of "disrememberin'", or doubts as to the number—doubts never laid except by a double count. In the first, so intent was the man, that he forgot his mate; though his relief in being good friends again had made him ignore his fear.

But the dog had heard an outside sound, and, moving to the door, waited for certainty. At this stage the man missed his mate's eyes.

He lay face downward, covering his treasure, when he realized that his friend was uneasy. And as the dog kept watch, he thrust them back hurriedly, missing all the pleasure and excitement of a final recount.

With dumb show he asked several questions of his sentinel, and took his answers from his eyes. Then, when Warder, relieved, began to walk about, the old man with forced confidence chaffed him. He sought refuge from his own fears by trying to banish the dog's, and suggested dingoes at the sheepyard, or a "goanner" on the roof. "Well, 'twas 'possum," he said, making a pretence of even then hearing and distinguishing the sound.

But round his waist the belt did not go that night. Only its bulk in his life of solitariness could have conceived its hiding place.

He bustled around as one having many tasks, but these he did aimlessly. With a pretence of unconcern he attempted to hum, but broke off frequently to listen. He was plainly afraid of the dog's keen ears missing something. But his mate's tense body proclaimed him on duty.

"I know who yer thort 'twas, Warder!" They were sitting side by side, yet he spoke very loudly. "Scrammy 'and, ehm?" He had guessed correctly.

"An' yer thort yer see 'im lars' night!" He was right again.

"An' yer thort 'twas 'im that 'ad bin ramsakin' the place yesterday, when we was shepherdin'. An' yer thort 't must 'ave bin 'im shook the tommy!" The dog's manner evinced that he had not altered this opinion. The old man's heart beat loudly.

"No fear, Warder! Scrammy's gone, gone long ways now, Warder!" But Warder's pricked ears doing double duty showed he was unconvinced. " 'Sides, Scrammy wouldn't 'urt er merskeeter," he continued. "Poor ole Scrammy! 'Twarn't 'im shook the tommy, Warder!" The dog seemed to be waiting for the suggestion of another thief having unseen crept into their isolated lives, but his master had none to offer. Both were silent, then the man piled wood on the fire, remarking that he was going to sit up all night. He asked the dog to go with him to the table to feed and trim the slush-lamp.

Those quavering shadows along the wall were caused by its sizzling flare flickering in the darkness, the dog explained. "Thort it mighter bin ther blacks outside," the man said. "They ain't so fur away, I know! 'Twar them killed ther lamb down in ther creek." He spoke unusually loudly. He hoped they wouldn't catch "poor ole one-'anded Scrammy". He said how sorry he was for "poor ole Scrammy, cos Scrammy wouldn't 'urt no one. He on'y jes' came ter see us cos 'e was a ole friend. He was gone along ways ter look fur work, cos 'e was stony broke after blueing 'is cheque at ther shanty sixty miles away."

"I tole 'im," he continued in an altered voice, "thet I

couldn't lend 'im eny cos I 'ad sent all my little bit er money" (he whispered "money") "to ther bank be ther boss. Didn' I?" Emphatically his mate intimated that this was the case. He held his head in his shaking hands, and complained to the dog of having "come over dizzy".

He was silent for a few moments, then, abruptly raising his voice, he remarked that their master was a better tracker than "Saddle-strap Jimmy", or any of the blacks. He looked at the tally stick, and suddenly announced that he knew for a certainty that the boss and his wife would return that night or early next morning, and that he must see about making them a damper. He got up and began laboriously to mix soda and salt with the flour. He looked at the muddy-coloured water in the bucket near the wall, and altered his mind.

"I'll bile it first, War, same as 'er does, cos jus' neow an' then t' day I comes over dizzy-like. See th' mist t's even! Two more, then rain—rain, an' them two out in it without no tilt on the cart." He sat down for a moment, even before he dusted his ungoverned floury hands.

"Pint er tea, War, jes' t' warm ther worms an' lif' me 'art, eh!"

Every movement of the dog was in accord with this plan.

His master looked at the billy, and said, " 'twarn't bilin' ", and that a watched pot never boiled. He rested a while silently with his floury hands covering his face. He bent his mouth to the dog's ear and whispered. Warder, before replying, pointed his ears and raised his head. The old man's hand rested on the dog's neck.

"Tell yer wot, War, w'ile it's bilin' I'll 'ave another go at ther button, cos I want ter give 'im ther 'at soon as he comes. S'pose they'll orl come!" He had sat down again, and seemed to whistle his words. "Think they'll orl come, Loo?"

Loo would not commit himself about "orl", not being quite sure of his master's mind.

The old man's mouth twitched, a violent effort jerked him. "Might be a boy arter orl; ain't cocky sure!" His head wagged irresponsibly, and his hat fell off as he rolled into the bunk. He made no effort to replace it, and, for once unheeded, the fire flickered on his polished head. Never before had the dog seen its baldness. The change from night-cap to hat had always been effected out of his sight.

"War, ain't cocky sure it'll be a gal?"

The dog discreetly or modestly dropped his eyes, but his master had not done with concessions.

"Warder!" Warder looked at him. "Tell yer wot, you can go every Sunday evenin' an' see if 'tis a boy!"

He turned over on his side, with his face to the wall. Into the gnarled uncontrolled hand swaying over the bunk the dog laid his paw.

When the old man got up, he didn't put on his hat nor even pick it up. Altogether there was an unusualness about him tonight that distressed his mate. He sat up after a few moments, and threw back his head, listening strainingly for outside sounds. The silence soothed him, and he lay down again. A faded look was in his eyes.

"Thort I 'eard bells—church bells," he said to the dog looking up too, but at him. "Couldn't 'ave. No church bells in the bush. Ain't 'eard 'em since I lef' th' ole country." He turned his best ear to the fancied sound. He had left his dog and the hut, and was dreaming of shadowy days.

He raised himself from the bunk, and followed the dog's eyes to a little smoke-stained bottle on the shelf. "No, no, War!" he said. "Thet's for sickness; mus' be a lot worser'n wot I am!" Breathing noisily, he went through a list of diseases, among which were palsy, snake-bite, "dropersy", and "suddint death", before he would be justified in taking the last of his pain-killer.

His pipe was in his hidden belt, but he had another in one of those little pockets. He tried it, said " 'twouldn't draw'r", and very slowly and clumsily stripped the edge of a cabbage-tree frond hanging from the rafter, and tried to push it through the stem, but could not find the opening. He explained to the intent dog that the hole was stopped up, but it didn't matter. He placed it under the bunk where he sat, because first he would " 'ave a swig er tea". His head kept wagging at the billy. No, until the billy boiled he was going to have a little snooze. The dog was to keep quiet until the billy boiled.

Involuntarily he murmured, looking at his mate, "Funny w'ere ther tommy'awk's gone ter!" Then he missed the axe. "My Gord, Warder!" he said, "I lef' the axe outside; clean forgot it!" This discovery alarmed the dog, and he suggested they should bring it in.

"No, no!" he said, and his floury face grew ghastly.

He stood still; all his faculties seemed paralysed for a time, then fell stiffly on his bunk. Quite suddenly he staggered to his feet, rubbed his eyes, and between broken breaths he complained of the bad light, and that the mist had come again.

One thing the dog did when he saw his master's face even by that indifferent light, he barked low, and terribly human.

The old man motioned for silence. "Ah!" His jaw fell but only for a moment. Then a steely grimness took possession. He clung to the table and beckoned the dog with one crooked finger. "Scrammy?" cunningly, cautiously, indicating outside, and as subtly the dog replied. Then he groped for his bunk, and lay with his eyes fixed on the billy, his mouth open.

He brought his palms together after a while. " 'Cline our 'earts ter keep this lawr," he whispered, and for a moment his eyes rested on the hiding place, then turned to the dog.

And though soon after there was a sinister sound outside, which the watchful dog immediately challenged, the man on the bunk lay undisturbed.

Warder, growling savagely, went along the back wall of the hut, and, despite the semi-darkness, his eyes scintillating with menace through the cracks drove from them a crouching figure who turned hastily to grip the axe near the myall logs. He stumbled over the lamb's feeding-pan lying in the hut's shadow. The moonlight glittering on the blade recalled the menace of the dog's eyes. The man grabbed the weapon swiftly, but even with it he felt the chances were unequal.

But he had planned to fix the dog. He would unpen the sheep, and the lurking dingoes, coming up from the creek to worry the lambs, would prove work for the dog. He crouched silently to again deceive this man and dog, and crept towards the sheepyard. But the hurdles of the yard faced the hut, and the way those thousand eyes reflected the rising moon was disconcerting. The whole of the night seemed pregnant with eyes.

All the shadows were slanting the wrong way, and the moon was facing him, with its man calmly watching every movement. It would be dawn before it set. He backed from the yard to the myall's scant screen. Even they had moulted with age. From under his coat the handle of the axe protruded. His mind worked his body. Hugging the axe, he crept towards some object, straightened himself to reach, then with the hook on his handless arm, drew back an imaginary bolt, and stooping entered. With the axe in readiness he crept to the bunk. Twice he raised it and struck.

It was easy enough out there, yet even in imagination his skin was wet and his mouth was dry. Even if the man slept, there was the dog. He must risk letting out the sheep. He covered the blade of the axe and went in a circuit to the sheep, and got over the yard on the side opposite to the hut. They rushed from him and huddled together, leaving him, although stooping, exposed. He had calculated for this, but not for the effect upon himself. Could they in the hut see him, he would be no match for the dog even with the axe. Heedlessly, fear-driven, he rushed to where he could see the door, regardless of exposing himself. Nothing counted now, but that the dog or the old man should not steal upon him unawares.

The door was still closed. No call for "Warder!" came from it, though he stood there a conspicious object. While he watched he saw an ewe lamb make for the hut's shelter. He stooped, still watching, and listened, but could hear nothing. He crept forward and loosened the hurdles. Never were they noisier, he was sure. He knew that the sheep would not go through while he was there. He crept away, but although the leader noted the freed exit, he and those he led were creatures of habit. None were hungry, and they were unused to feeding at night, though in the morning, came man and dog never so early, they were waiting.

Round the yard and past the gateway he drove them again and again. He began to feel impotently frenzied in the fear that the extraordinary lightness meant that daylight must be near. Every moment he persuaded himself that he could see more plainly. He held out his one hand and was convinced.

He straightened himself, rushed among them, caught one, and ran it kicking through the opening. It came back the moment he freed it. However it served his purpose, for as he crouched there, baffled, he unexpectedly saw them file out. Then they rushed through in an impatient struggling crowd, each fearing to be last with this invader.

When he "barrowed" out the first, he had kept his eyes on the hut, and had seen an old ewe and lamb run to it and bunt the closed door. But if there was any movement inside, the noise of the nearer sheep killed it.

They were all round the hut, for above it hung the moon, and they all made for the light. He crept after them, his ears straining for sound, but his head bobbing above them to watch the still closed door.

Inside, long since, the back-log had split with an explosion that scattered the coals near enough to cause the billy to boil, and the blaze showed the old man's eyes set on the billy. The dog looked into them, then laid his head between his paws, and, still watching his master's face, beat the ground with his tail. He whined softly and went back to his post at the door, his eyes snapping flintily, his teeth bared. Along his back the hair rose like bristles. He sent an assurance of help to the importunate ewe and lamb. As the sheep neared the hut, he ran to the bunk, raised his head to a level with his master's, and barked softly. He waited, and despite the eager light in his intelligent face, his master and mate did not ask him any questions as to the cause of these calling sheep. Why did he not rise, and with him re-yard them, then gloatingly ask him where was the chinky crow by day, or sneaking dingo by night, that was any match for them, and then demand from his four-footed trusty mate the usual straightforward answer? Was there to be no discussion as to which heard the noise first, nor the final compromise of a dead-heat?

The silence puzzled the man outside sorely; he crouched, watching both door and shutter. The sheep were all round the hut. Man and dog inside must hear them. Why, when a dingo came that night he camped with them, they heard it before it could reach a lamb. If only he had known then what he knew now! His hold on the axe tightened. No one had seen him come; none should see him go! Why didn't that old fellow wake tonight? for now, as he crept nearer the hut, he could hear the whining dog, and under-stood, he was appealing to his master.

He lay flat on the ground and tried to puzzle it out. The sheep had rushed back disorganized and were again near the hut and yard. Both inside must know. They were waiting for him. They were preparing for him, and that was why they were letting the dingoes play up with the sheep. That was the reason they did not openly show fight.

Still he would have sacrificed half of the coveted wealth to be absolutely certain of what their silence meant. It was surely almost daylight. He spread out the fingers of his one hand; he could see the colour of the blood in the veins. He must act quickly, or he would have to hide about for another day. And the absent man might return. To encourage himself, he tried to imagine the possession of that glittering heap that he had seen them counting on the mat. Yet he had grown cold and dejected, and felt for the first time the weight of the axe. It would be all right if the door would open, the old man come out and send the dog to round up the sheep. It was getting daylight, and soon shelter would be impossible.

He crept towards the hut, and this time he felt the edge of the axe. Right and left the sheep parted. There was nothing to be gained now in crawling, for the hostility of the dog told him that he could be seen. He stood, his body stiffened with determination.

Mechanically he went to the door; he knew the defensive resources of the hut. He had the axe, and the stolen toma-hawk was stuck in the fork of those myalls. He had no need for both. The only weapon that the old fellow had was the useless butcher's knife. His eyes protruded, and uncon-sciously he felt his stiffened beard.

He breathed without movement. There was no sound now from man or dog. In his mind he saw them waiting for him to attack the door; this he did not debate nor alter.

G

He went to the shutter, ran the axe's edge along the hide
hinges, pushed it in, then stepped back.

Immediately the dog's head appeared. He growled no
protest, but the flinty fire from his eyes and the heat of his
suppressed breath, hissing between his bared fangs, revealed
to Scrammy that in this contest, despite the axe, his one
hand was a serious handicap.

With the first blow his senses quickened. The slush-
lamp had gone out and there was no hint of daylight
inside. This he noted between his blows at the dog, as he
looked for his victim. It was strange the old fellow did
not show fight! Where was he hiding? Was it possible that,
scenting danger, he had slipped out? He recalled the
dog's warning when his master was counting his hoard.
The memory of that chinking belt-hidden pile dominated
greedily. Had the old man escaped? He would search the
hut; what were fifty dogs' teeth? In close quarters he would
do for him with one blow.

He was breathing now in deep gasps. The keen edge
of the axe severed the hide-hinged door. He rushed it; then
stood back swinging the axe in readiness. It did not fall,
for the bolt still held it. But this was only what a child
would consider a barrier. One blow with the axe-head
smashed the bolt. The door fell across the head of the
bunk, the end partly blocking the entrance. He struck
a side blow that sent it along the bunk.

The dog was dreadfully distressed. The bushman outside
thought the cause the fallen door. Face to face they met—
determined battle in the dog's eyes met murder in the
man's. He brandished an axe circuit, craned his neck, and
by the dull light of the fire searched the hut. He saw no
one but the dog. Unless his master was under the bunk, he
had escaped. The whole plot broke on him quite suddenly!
The cunning old miser, knowing his dog would show his
flight by following, had locked him in, and he had wasted

all this time barking up the wrong tree. He would have done the old man to death that minute with fifty brutal blows. He would kill him by day or night.

He ran round the brush sheepyard, kicking and thrusting the axe through the thickest parts. He had not hidden there, nor among the myall clump where he had practised his bloody plot. The dog stood at the doorway of the hut. He saw this as he passed through the sheep on his way to search the creek. He was half minded to try to invite the dog's confidence and cooperation by yarding them.

He looked at them, and the moonlight's undulating white scales across their shorn backs brought out the fresh tar brand 8, setting him thinking of the links of that convict gang chain long ago. Lord, how light it must be for him to see that!

He held out his hand again. There was no perceptible change in the light. There were hours yet before daylight. He moulded his mind to that.

The creek split the plain, and along it here and there a few sheoak blots defined it. He traversed it with his eyes. There were no likely hiding places among the trees, and it would be useless to search them. Suddenly it struck him that the old man might be creeping along with the sheep—they were so used to him. He ran and headed them, driving them swiftly back to the yard. Before they were in he knew he was wrong. Again he turned and scanned the creek, but felt no impulse to search it. It was half a mile from the hut. It was impossible that the old man could have got there, or that he could have reached the more distant house. Besides, why did the dog stay at the door unless on guard? He ran back to the hut.

The dog was still there, and in no way appeased by the yarding of the sheep. He swore at the threatening brute, and cast about for a gibber to throw, but stones were almost unknown there. A sapling would serve him! Seven or eight

myall logs lay near for firewood, but all were too thick to
be wielded. There was only the clump of myalls, and the
few stunted sheoaks bordering the distant creek. To reach
either would mean a dangerous delay. Oh, by God, he had
it! These poles keeping down the bark roof. He ran to the
back of the hut, cut a step in a slab, and, putting his foot
in it, hitched the axe on one of the desired poles and was
up in a moment. He could hear the cabbage fronds hanging from the rafters shiver with the vibration, but there
was no other protest from inside.

He shifted a sheet of rotten bark; part of it crumbled
and fell inside on the prostrate door, sounding like the first
earth on a coffin, in a way that the dog particularly resented.
He knelt and carefully eyed the interior. The dog's glittering
eyes met his. The door lay as it had fallen along the bunk.
The fire was lightless, yet he could see more plainly, but
the cause was not manifest, till from the myalls quite close
the jackasses chorused. From his post the dog sent them
a signal. Quite unaccountably the man's muscles relaxed.
"Oh, Christ!" he said, dropping the pole. He sprang up
and faced the East, then turned to the traitorous faded
moon. The daylight had come.

The sweat stung his quivering body. Slowly, he made an
eye circuit round the plain; no human being was in sight.
All he had to face was a parcel of noisy jackasses and a
barking dog! He would soon silence the dog. He took
the pole and made a jab at the whelping brute. One thing
he noticed, that if he did get one home, it was only when
he worked near the horizontal door. His quickened senses
guessed at the reason. He could have shifted the door
easily with his pole, yet feared, because, if the old man
were under, he would expose himself to two active enemies.
He must get to close quarters with the dog, and chop him
in two, or brain him with the axe.

He ripped off another sheet of bark, and smashed away

a batten that broke his swing. Encircling a rafter with his hooked arm, he lay flat, his feet pressing another just over the bunk, because only there would the dog hold his ground. One blow well directed got home. He planted his feet firmly, and made another with such tremendous force that his support snapped. He let go the axe and it fell on the door. He gripped with his hand the rafter nearest, but strain as he would he could not balance his body. He hung over the door, and the dog sprang at him and dragged him down. In bitten agony, he dropped on the door that instantly up-ended.

It was daylight, and in that light the power of those open eyes set in that bald head, fixed on the billy beside the dead fireplace, was mightier than the dog. His unmaimed hand had the strength of both. He lifted the door and shielded himself with it as he backed out.

But that was not all the dog wanted. At the doorway he waited to see that the fleeing man had no further designs on the sheep.

It was time they were feeding. Though the hurdles were down, even from the doorway, the dog was their master. He waited for commands from his, and barked them back till noon.

Several times that day the ewe and lamb came in, looked without speculation at the figure on the bunk, then moved to the dead fireplace. But though the water in the billy was cold, the dog would not allow either to touch it. That was for tea when his master awoke.

There was another circumstance. Those blowflies were welcome to the uncovered mutton. Throughout that day he gave them undisputed right, but they had to be content with it.

Next day the ewe and lamb came again. The lamb bunted several irresponsive objects—never its dam's udder —baaing listlessly. Though the first day the ewe had looked at the bunk, and baaed, she was wiser now, though sheep are slow to learn. Around that dried dish outside the lamb sniffed, baaing faintly. Adroitly the ewe led the way to the creek, and the lamb followed. From the bank the lamb looked at her, then faced round to the hut, and, baaing disconsolately, trotted a few paces back. From the water's edge the mother ewe called. The lamb looked at her vacantly, and without interest descended. The ewe bent and drank sparingly, meaningly. The lamb sniffed the water, and, unsatisfied, complained. The hut was hidden, but it turned that way. Again the ewe leisurely drank. This time the lamb's lips touched the water, but did not drink. Into its mouth raised to bleat a few drops fell. Hastily the mother's head went to the water. She did not drink, but the lamb did. Higher up, where the creek was dry, they crossed to tender grass in the billabong, then joined the flock for the first time.

Through the thicker mist that afternoon a white tilted cart sailed joltingly, taking its bearings from the various landmarks rather than from the undefined track. It rounded the scrub, and the woman, with her baby, kept watch for the first glimpse of her home beyond the creek. She told her husband that there was no smoke from the nearer shepherd's hut, but despite his uneasiness he tried to persuade her that the mist absorbed it.

It was past sundown, yet the straggling unguarded sheep were running in mobs to and from the creek. Both saw the broken roof of the hut, and the man, stopping the horse some distance away, gave the woman the reins and bade her wait. He entered the hut through the broken doorway, but immediately came out to assure himself that his wife had not moved.

The sight inside of that broken-ribbed dog's fight with those buzzing horrors, and the reproach in his wild eyes, was a memory that the man was not willing she should share.

Billy Skywonkie

THE line was unfenced, so with due regard to the possibility of the drought-dulled sheep attempting to chew it, the train crept cautiously along, stopping occasionally, without warning, to clear it from the listless starving brutes. In the carriage nearest the cattle-vans, some drovers and scrub-cutters were playing euchre, and spasmodically chorusing the shrill music from an uncertain concertina. When the train stopped, the player thrust his head from the carriage window. From one nearer the engine, a commercial traveller remonstrated with the guard, concerning the snail's pace and the many unnecessary halts.

"Take yer time, ole die-'ard," yelled the drover to the guard. "Whips er time—don't bust yerself fer no one. Wot's orl the worl' to a man w'en his wife's a widder." He laughed noisily and waved his hat at the seething bagman. "Go an' 'ave a snooze. I'll wake yer up ther day after termorrer."

He craned his neck to see into the nearest cattle-van. Four were down, he told his mates, who remarked, with blasphemous emphasis, that they would probably lose half before getting them to the scrub country.

The listening woman passenger, in a carriage between the drover and the bagman, heard a thud soon after in the cattle-truck, and added another to the list of the fallen.

Before dawn that day the train had stopped at a siding to truck them, and she had watched with painful interest these drought-tamed brutes being driven into the crowded vans. The tireless, greedy sun had swiftly followed the grey dawn, and in the light that even now seemed old and worn, the desolation of the barren shelterless plains, that the night had hidden, appalled her. She realized the sufferings of the emaciated cattle. It was barely noon, yet she had twice emptied the water bottle "shogging" in the iron bracket.

The train dragged its weary 'ength again, and she closed her eyes from the monotony of the dead plain. Suddenly the engine cleared its throat in shrill welcome to two iron tanks, hoisted twenty feet and blazing like evil eyes from a vanished face.

Beside them it squatted on its hunkers, placed a blackened thumb on its pipe, and hissed through its closed teeth like a snared wild-cat, while gulping yards of water. The green slimy odour penetrated to the cattle. The lustiest of these stamped feebly, clashing their horns and bellowing a hollow request.

A long-bearded bushman was standing on the few slabs that formed a siding, with a stockwhip coiled like a snake on his arm. The woman passenger asked him the name of the place.

"This is ther Never-Never—ther lars' place Gord made," answered one of the drovers who were crowding the windows.

"Better'n ther 'ell 'ole yous come from, any'ow," defended the bushman. "Breakin' ther 'earts, an' dyin' from suerside, cos they lef' it," he added derisively, pointing to the cattle.

In patriotic anger he passed to the guard-van without answering her question, though she looked anxiously after him. At various intervals during the many halts of the train, she had heard some of the obscene jokes, and with it in motion, snatches of lewd songs from the drovers' carriage. But the language used by this bushman to the guard, as he helped to remove a ton of fencing-wire topping his new saddle, made her draw back her head. Near the siding was a spring cart, and she presently saw him throw his flattened saddle into it and drive off. There was no one else in sight, and in nervous fear she asked the bagman if this was Gooriabba siding. It was nine miles further, he told her.

The engine lifted its thumb from its pipe. "Well—well—to—be—sure; well—well—to—be—sure," it puffed, as if in shocked remembrance of its being hours late for its appointment there.

She saw no one on the next siding, but a buggy waited near the sliprails. It must be for her. According to Sydney arrangements she was to be met here, and driven out twelve miles. A drover inquired as the train left her standing by her portmanteau, "Are yer travellin' on yer lonesome, or on'y goin' somew'ere!" and another flung a twist of paper towards her, brawling unmusically, that it was "A flowwer from me angel mother's ger-rave."

She went towards the buggy, but as she neared it the driver got in and made to drive off. She ran and called, for when he went she would be alone with the bush all round her, and only the sound of the hoarse croaking of the frogs from the swamp near, and the raucous "I'll—'ave—'is—eye—out", of the crows.

Yes, he was from Gooriabba Station, and had come to meet a young "piece" from Sydney, who had not come.

She was ghastly with bilious sickness—the result of an over-fed brain and an under-fed liver. Her face flushed muddily. "Was it a housekeeper?"

He was the rouseabout, wearing his best clothes with awful unusualness. The coat was too long in the sleeve, and wrinkled across the back with his bush slouch. There was that wonderful margin of loose shirt between waist-coat and trousers, which all swagger bushies affect. Subordinate to nothing decorative was the flaring silk handkerchief, drawn into a sailor's knot round his neck.

He got out and fixed the winkers, then put his hands as far as he could reach into his pockets—from the position of his trousers he could not possibly reach bottom. It was apparently some unknown law that suspended them. He thrust forward his lower jaw, elevated his pipe, and squirted a little tobacco juice towards his foot that was tracing semicircles in the dust. "Damned if I know," he said with a snort, "but there'll be a 'ell of a row somew'ere."

She noticed that the discoloured teeth his bush grin showed so plainly, were worn in the centre, and met at both sides with the pipe between the front. Worn stepping-stones, her mind insisted.

She looked away towards the horizon where the smoke of the hidden train showed faintly against a clear sky, and as he was silent, she seemed to herself to be intently listening to the croak of the frogs and the threat of the crows. She knew that, from under the brim of the hat he wore over his eyes, he was looking at her sideways.

Suddenly he withdrew his hands and said again, "Damned if I know. S'pose it's all right! Got any traps? Get up then an' 'ole the Neddy while I get it." They drove a mile or so in silence; his pipe was still in his mouth though not alight.

She spoke once only. "What a lot of frogs seem to be in that lake!"

He laughed. "That's ther Nine Mile Dam!" He laughed again after a little—an intelligent, complacent laugh.

"It used ter be swarmin' with teal in a good season, but Gord A'mighty knows w'en it's ever goin' ter rain any more! I dunno!" This was an important admission, for he was a great weather prophet. "Lake!" he sniggered and looked sideways at his companion. "Thet's wot thet there bloke, the painter doodle, called it. An' 'e goes ter dror it, an' 'e sez wot 'e 'll give me five bob if I'll run up ther horses, an' keep 'em so's 'e ken put 'em in ther picshure. An' 'e drors ther Dam an' ther trees, puts in thet there ole dead un, an' 'e puts in ther 'orses right clost against ther water w'ere the frogs is. 'E puts them in too, an' damned if 'e don't dror ther 'orses drinkin' ther water with ther frogs, an' ther frogs' spit on it! Likely yarn ther 'orses ud drink ther water with ther blanky frogs' spit on it! Fat lot they know about ther bush! Blarsted nannies!"

Presently he inquired as to the place where they kept pictures in Sydney, and she told him, the Art Gallery.

"Well some of these days I'm goin' down ter Sydney," he continued, "an' I'll collar thet one 'cos it's a good likerness of ther 'orses—you'd know their 'ide on a gum-tree—an' that mean mongrel never paid me ther five bob."

Between his closed teeth he hissed a bush tune for some miles, but ceased to look at the sky, and remarked, "No sign er rain! No lambin' this season; soon as they're dropt we'll 'ave ter knock 'em all on ther 'ead!" He shouted an oath of hatred at the crows following after the tottering sheep that made in a straggling line for the water. "Look at 'em!" he said. "Scoffin' out ther eyes!" He pointed to where the crows hovered over the bogged sheep. "They putty well lives on eyes! 'Blanky bush Chinkies!' I call 'em. No one carn't tell 'em apart!"

There was silence again, except for a remark that he could spit all the blanky rain they had had in the last nine months.

Away to the left along a side track his eyes travelled searchingly, as they came to a gate. He stood in the buggy and looked again.

"Promised ther 'Konk' t' leave 'im 'ave furst squint at yer," he muttered, "if 'e was 'ere t' open ther gate! But I'm not goin' t' blanky well wait orl day!" He reluctantly got out and opened the gate, and he had just taken his seat when a "Coo-ee" sounded from his right, heralded by a dusty pillar. He snorted resentfully. " 'Ere 'e is; jes' as I got out an' done it!"

The Konk cantered to them, his horse's hoofs padded by the dust-cushioned earth. The driver drew back, so as not to impede the newcomer's view. After a moment or two, the Konk, preferring closer quarters, brought his horse round to the left. Unsophisticated bush wonder in the man's face met the sophisticated in the girl's.

Never had she seen anything so grotesquely monkeyish. And the nose of this little hairy horror, as he slewed his neck to look into her face, blotted the landscape and dwarfed all perspective. She experienced a strange desire to extend her hand. When surprise lessened, her mettle saved her from the impulse to cover her face with both hands, to baffle him.

At last the silence was broken by the driver drawing a match along his leg, and lighting his pipe. The hairy creature safely arranged a pair of emu eggs, slung with bush skill round his neck.

"Ain't yer goin' to part?" enquired the driver, indicating his companion as the recipient.

"Wot are yer givin' us; wot do yer take me fur?" said the Konk indignantly, drawing down his knotted veil.

"Well, give 'em ter me fer Lizer."

"Will yer 'ave 'em now, or wait till yer get 'em?"

"Goin' ter sit on 'em yerself?" sneered the driver.

"Yes, an' I'll give yer ther first egg ther cock lays," laughed the Konk.

He turned his horse's head back to the gate. "I say, Billy Skywonkie! Wot price Sally Ah Too, eh?" he asked, his gorilla mouth agape.

Billy Skywonkie uncrossed his legs, took out the whip. He tilted his pipe and shook his head as he prepared to drive, to show that he understood to a fraction the price of Sally Ah Too. The aptness of the question took the sting out of his having had to open the gate. He gave a farewell jerk.

"Goin' ter wash yer neck?" shouted the man with the nose, from the gate.

"Not if I know it."

The Konk received the intimation incredulously. "Stinkin' Roger!" he yelled. In bush parlance this was equal to emphatic disbelief.

This was a seemingly final parting, and both started, but suddenly the Konk wheeled round.

"Oh, Billy!" he shouted.

Billy stayed his horse and turned expectantly.

"W'en's it goin' ter rain?"

The driver's face darkened. "Your blanky jealersey 'll get yer down, an' worry yer yet," he snarled, and slashing his horse he drove rapidly away.

"Mickey ther Konk," he presently remarked to his companion, as he stroked his nose.

This explained her earlier desire to extend her hand. If the Konk had been a horse she would have stroked his nose.

"Mob er sheep can camp in the shadder of it," he said.

Boundless scope for shadows on that sun-smitten treeless plain!

"Make a good plough-shere," he continued, "easy plough a cultivation paddock with it!"

At the next gate he seemed in a mind and body conflict. There were two tracks; he drove along one for a few hundred yards. Then stopping, he turned, and finding the Konk out of sight, abruptly drove across to the other. He continually drew his whip along the horse's back, and haste seemed the object of the movement, though he did not flog the beast.

After a few miles on the new track, a blob glittered

dazzlingly through the glare, like a fallen star. It was the iron roof of the wine shanty—the Saturday night and Sunday resort of shearers and rouseabouts for twenty miles around. Most of its spirits was made on the premises from bush recipes, of which bluestone and tobacco were the chief ingredients. Every drop had the reputation of "bitin' orl ther way down".

A sapling studded with broken horse-shoes seemed to connect two lonely crow stone trees. Under their scanty shade groups of dejected fowls stood with beaks agape. Though the buggy wheels almost reached them, they were motionless but for quivering gills. The ground both sides of the shanty was decorated with tightly-pegged kangaroo-skins. A dog, apathetically blind and dumb, lay on the veranda, lifeless save for eyelids blinking in antagonism to the besieging flies.

"Jerry can't be far off," said Billy Skywonkie, recognizing the dog. He stood up in the buggy. "By cripes, there 'e is —goosed already, an' 'e on'y got 'is cheque lars' night."

On the chimney side of the shanty a man lay in agitated sleep beside his rifle and swag. There had been a little shade on that side in the morning, and he had been sober enough to select it, and lay his head on his swag. He had emptied the bottle lying at his feet since then. His swag had been thoroughly "gone through", and also his singlet and trouser-pockets. The fumes from the shanty grog baffled the flies. But the scorching sun was conquering; the man groaned, and his hands began to search for his burning head.

Billy Skywonkie explained to his companion that it was "thet fool, Jerry ther kangaroo-shooter, bluein' 'is cheque fer skins". He took the water bag under the buggy, and poured the contents into the open mouth and over the face of the "dosed" man, and raised him into a sitting posture. Jerry fought this friendliness vigorously, and, staggering to his feet, picked up his rifle, and took drunken aim at his rescuer, then at the terrified woman in the buggy.

The rouseabout laughed unconcernedly. " 'E thinks we're blanky kangaroos," he said to her. "Jerry, ole cock, yer couldn't 'it a woolshed! Yer been taking ther sun!"

He took the rifle and pushed the subdued Jerry into the chimney corner.

He tilted his hat, till, bush fashion, it " 'ung on one 'air", and went inside the shanty. "Mag!" he shouted, thumping the bar (a plank supported by two casks). ˙

The woman in the buggy saw a slatternly girl with doughy hands come from the back, wiping the flour from her face with a kitchen towel. They made some reference to her she knew, as the girl came to the door and gave her close scrutiny. Then, shaking her head till her long brass earrings swung like pendulums, she laughed loudly.

"Eh?" enquired the rouseabout.

"My oath! Square dinkum!" she answered, going behind the bar.

He took the silk handkerchief from his neck, and playfully tried to flick the corner into her eye. Mag was used to such delicate attentions and well able to defend herself. With the dirty kitchen towel she succeeded in knocking off his hat, and round and round the house she ran with it dexterously dodging the skin-pegs. He could neither overtake nor outwit her with any dodge. He gave in, and ransomed his hat with the "shouts" she demanded.

From the back of the shanty, a bent old woman, almost on all fours, crept towards the man, again prostrate in the corner. She paused, with her ear turned to where the girl and the rouseabout were still at horse-play. With cat-like movements she stole on till within reach of Jerry's empty pockets. She turned her terrible face to the woman in the buggy, as if in expectation of sympathy. Keeping wide of the front door, she came to the further side of the buggy.

With the fascination of horror the woman looked at this creature, whose mouth and eyes seemed to dishonour her draggled grey hair. She was importuning for something, but the woman in the buggy could not understand till she pointed to her toothless mouth (the mission of which seemed to be, to fill its cavernous depths with the age-loosened skin above and below). A blue bag under each eye aggressively ticked like the gills of the fowls, and the sinews of the neck strained into *basso-rilievo*. Alternately she pointed to her mouth, or laid her knotted fingers on the blue bags in pretence of wiping tears. Entrenched behind the absorbed skin-terraces, a stump of purple tongue made efforts at speech. When she held out her claw, the woman understood and felt for her purse. Wolfishly the old hag snatched and put into her mouth the coin, and as the now merry driver, followed by Mag, came, she shook a warning claw at the giver, and flopped whining in the dust, her hands ostentatiously open and wiping dry eyes.

" 'Ello Biddy, on ther booze again!"

The bottle bulging from his coat pocket made speech with him intelligible, despite the impeding coin.

He placed the bottle in the boot of the buggy, and, turning to Mag, said "Give ther poor ole cow a dose!"

"Yes, one in a billy; anything else might make her sick!" said Mag. "I caught 'er jus' now swiggin' away with ther tap in 'er mug!"

He asked his companion would she like a wet. She asked for water, and so great was her need that, making a barricade of closed lips and teeth to the multitude of apparently wingless mosquitoes thriving in its green tepidity, she moistened her mouth and throat.

"Oh, I say, Billy!" called Mag as he drove off. Her tones suggested her having forgotten an important matter, and he turned eagerly. "W'en's it goin' ter rain?" she shrieked, convulsed with merriment.

"Go an' crawl inter a 'oller log!" he shouted angrily.

"No, but truly, Billy?"

Billy turned again. "Give my love to yaller Lizer; thet slues yer!"

They had not gone far before he looked round again. "Gord!" he cried excitedly. "Look at Mag goin' through 'er ole woman!"

Mag had the old woman's head between her knees, dentist-fashion, and seemed to concentrate upon her victim's mouth, whose feeble impotence was soon demonstrated by the operator releasing her, and triumphantly raising her hand.

What the finger and thumb held the woman knew and the other guessed.

"By Gord. Eh! thet's prime; ain't it? No flies on Mag; not a fly!" he said, admiringly.

"See me an' 'er?" he asked, as he drove on.

His tone suggested no need to reply, and his listener did not. A giddy unreality took the sting from everything, even from her desire to beseech him to turn back to the siding, and leave her there to wait for the train to take her back to civilization. She felt she had lost her mental balance. Little matters became distorted, and the greater shrivelled.

He was now more communicative, and the oaths and adjectives so freely used were surely coined for such circumstances. "Damned" the wretched, starving, and starved sheep looked and were; "bloody" the beaks of the glutted crows; "blarsted" the whole of the plain they drove through!

Gaping cracks suggested yawning graves, and the skeleton fingers of the drooping myalls seemingly pointed to them.

"See me an' Mag?" he asked again. "No flies on Mag; not a wink 'bout 'er!" He chuckled in tribute. "Ther wus thet damned flash fool, Jimmy Fernatty," he continued "—ther blanky fool; 'e never 'ad no show with Mag. An' yet 'e'd go down there! It wus two mile furder this way, yet damned if ther blanky fool wouldn't come this way every time, 'less ther boss 'e wus with 'im, 'stead er goin' ther short cut—ther way I come this mornin'. An' every time Mag ud make 'im part 'arf a quid! I was on'y there jus' 'bout five minits meself, an' I stuck up nea'ly 'arf a quid! An' there's four gates" (he flogged the horse and painted them crimson when he remembered them) "this way, more'n on ther way I come this mornin'."

Presently he gave her the reins with instructions to drive through one. It seemed to take a long time to close it, and he had to fix the back of the buggy before he opened it, and after it was closed.

After getting out several times in quick succession to fix the back of the buggy when there was no gate, he seemed to forget the extra distance. He kept his hand on hers when she gave him the reins, and bade her "keep up 'er pecker". "Someone would soon buck up ter 'er if their boss wusn't on." But the boss it seemed was a "terrer for young uns. Jimmy Fernatty 'as took up with a yaller piece an' is livin' with 'er. But not me; thet's not me! I'm like ther boss, thet's me! No yeller satin for me!"

He watched for the effect of this degree of taste on her.

Though she had withdrawn her hand, he kept winking at her, and she had to move her feet to the edge of the buggy to prevent his pressing against them. He told her with sudden anger that any red black-gin was as good as a half chow any day, and it was no use gammoning for he knew what she was.

"If Billy Skywonkie 'ad ter string onter yaller Lizer, more 'air on 'is chest fer doin' so" (striking his own). "I ken get as many w'ite gins as I wanter, an' I'd as soon tackle a gin as a chow anyways!"

On his next visit to the back of the buggy she heard the crash of glass breaking against a tree. After a few snatches of song he lighted his pipe, and grew sorrowfully reminiscent.

"Yes s'elp me, nea'ly 'arf a quid! An' thet coloured ole 'og of a cow of a mother, soon's she's off ther booze, 'll see thet she gets it!" Then he missed his silk handkerchief. "Ghost!" he said, breathing heavily, "Mag's snavelled it! Lizer 'll spot thet's gone soon's we get 'ithin coo-ee of 'er!"

Against hope he turned and looked along the road; felt every pocket, lifted his feet, and looked under the mat. His companion, in reply, said she had not seen it since his visit to the shanty.

"My Gord!" he said, "Mag's a fair terror!" He was greatly troubled till the braggart in him gave an assertive flicker. "Know wot I'll do ter Lizer soon's she begins ter start naggin' at me?" He intended this question as an insoluble conundrum, and waited for no surmises. "Fill 'er mug with this!" The shut fist he shook was more than a mugful. " 'Twouldn' be ther first time I done it, nor ther lars'." But the anticipation seemed little comfort to him.

The rest of the journey was done in silence, and without even a peep at the sky. When they came to the homestead gate he said his throat felt as though a "goanner" had crawled into it and died. He asked her for a pin and clumsily dropped it in his efforts to draw the collar up to his ears, but had better luck with a hair-pin.

He appeared suddenly subdued and sober, and as he took his seat after closing the gate, he offered her his hand, and said, hurriedly, "No 'arm done, an' no 'arm meant; an' don't let on ter my missus—thet's 'er on the verander—thet we come be ther shanty."

It was dusk, but through it she saw that the woman was dusky too.

"Boss in, Lizer?" There was contrition and propitiation in his voice.

"You've bin a nice blanky time," said his missus, "an' lucky fer you, Billy Skywonkie, 'e ain't."

With bowed head, his shoulders making kindly efforts

to hide his ears, he sat silent and listening respectfully. The woman in the buggy thought that the volubility of the angry half-caste's tongue was the nearest thing to perpetual motion. Under her orders both got down, and from a seat under the open window in the little room to which Lizer had motioned, she gave respectful attention to the still rapidly flowing tirade. The offence had been some terrible injustice to a respectable married woman, slavin' an' graftin' an' sweatin' from mornin' ter night, for a slungin' idlin' lazy blaggard." In an indefinable way the woman felt that both of them were guilty, and to hide from her part of the reproof was mean and cowardly. The half-caste from time to time included her, and by degrees she understood that the wasted time of which Lizer complained was supposed to have been dissipated in flirtation. Neither the shanty nor Mag had mention.

From a kitchen facing the yard a Chinaman came at intervals, and with that assumption of having mastered the situation in all its bearings through his thorough knowledge of the English tongue, he shook his head in calm, shocked surprise. His sympathies were unmistakably with Lizer, and he many times demonstrated his grip of the grievance by saying, "By Cli' Billy, it's a bloo'y shame!"

Maybe it was a sense of what was in his mind that made the quivering woman hide her face when virtuous Ching Too came to look at her. She was trying to eat when a dog ran into the dining-room, and despite the violent beating of her heart, she heard the rouseabout tell the boss as he unsaddled his horse, "The on'y woman I see was a 'alf chow, an' she ses she's the one, an' she's in ther dinin'-room 'avin' a tuck-in."

She was too giddy to stand when the boss entered, but she turned her mournful eyes on him, and, supporting herself by the table, stood and faced him.

He kept on his hat, and she, watching, saw curiosity and surprise change into anger as he looked at her.

"What an infernal cheek *you* had to come! Who sent you?" he asked stormily.

She told him, and added that she had no intention of remaining.

"How old?" She made no reply. His last thrust, as in disgust he strode out, had the effect of a galvanic battery on her dying body.

Her bedroom was reeking with a green heavy scent. Empty powder-boxes and rouge-pots littered the dressing-table, and various other aids to nature evidenced her predecessor's frailty. From a coign in its fastness a black spider eyed her malignantly, and as long as the light lasted she watched it.

The ringing of a bell slung outside in the fork of a tree awoke her before dawn. It was mustering—bush stock-taking—and all the stationhands were astir. There was a noise of galloping horses being driven into the stockyard, and the clamour of the men as they caught and saddled them. Above the clatter of plates in the kitchen she could hear the affected drawl of the Chinaman talking to Lizer. She trod heavily along the passage, preparing the boss's breakfast. This early meal was soon over, and with the dogs snapping playfully at the horses' heels, all rode off.

Spasmodic bars of "A Bicycle Built for Two" came from the kitchen, "Mayly, Mayly, give me answer do!" There was neither haste nor anxiety in the singer's tones. Before the kitchen fire, oblivious to the heat, stood the Chinaman cook, inert from his morning's opium. It was only nine, but this was well on in the day for Ching, whose morning began at four.

He ceased his song as she entered. "You come Sydiney? Ah! You mally? Ah! Sydiney welly ni' place. This placee welly dly—too muchee no lain—welly dly."

She was watching his dog. On a block lay a flitch of bacon, and across the freshly cut side the dog drew its tongue, then snapped at the flies. "That dog will eat the bacon," she said.

"No!" answered the cook. " 'E no eat 'em—too saw."

It *was* salt; she had tried it for breakfast.

He began energetically something about, "by an' by me getty mally. By Cli' no 'alf cas—too muchee longa jlaw." He laughed and shook his head, reminiscent of "las' a night", and waited for applause. But, fascinated, she still watched the dog, who from time to time continued to take "saw" with his flies.

"Go ou' si', Sir," said the cook in a spirit of rivalry. The dog stood and snapped. "Go ou' si', I say!" No notice from the dog. "Go ou' si', I tella you!" stamping his slippered feet and taking a fire-stick. The dog leisurely sat down and looked at his master with mild reproof. "Go insi' then, any bloo'y si' you li'!" but pointing to their joint bedroom with the lighted stick. The dog went to the greasy door, saw that the hens sitting on the bed were quietly laying eggs to go with the bacon, and came back.

She asked him where was the rouseabout who had driven her in yesterday.

"Oh, Billy Skywonkie, 'e mally alri'! Lizer 'im missie!" He went on to hint that affection there was misplaced, but that he himself was unattached.

She saw the rouseabout rattle into the yard in a spring cart. He let down the backboard and dumped three sheep under a light gallows. Their two front feet were strapped to one behind.

He seemed breathless with haste. "Oh, I say!" he called out to her. "Ther boss 'e tole me this mornin' thet I wus ter tell you, you wus ter sling yer 'ook. To do a get," he explained. "So bundle yer duds tergether quick an' lively! Lizer's down at ther tank, washin'. Le'ss get away afore she sees us, or she'll make yer swaller yer chewers." Lowering his voice, he continued: "I wanter go ter ther shanty—on'y ter get me 'ankerchief."

He bent and strained back a sheep's neck, drew the knife and steel from his belt, and skilfully danced an edge on the knife.

She noticed that the sheep lay passive, with its head back till its neck curved in a bow, and that the glitter of the knife was reflected in its eye.

Bush Church

Tʜᴇ hospitality of the bush never extends to the loan of a good horse to an inexperienced rider. The parson bumping along on old Rosey, who had smelt the water of the "Circler Dam", was powerless to keep the cunning experienced brute from diverting from the track. With the bit in her teeth, her pace kept him fully occupied to hold his seat. At the edge of the Dam, old Rosey, to avoid the treacherous mud, began, with humped back and hoofs close together, to walk along the plank that pier-wise extended to the deeper water. The parson's protests ended in his slipping over the arched neck of the wilful brute, on to the few inches of plank that she considerately left for him. The old mare drank leisurely, then backed off with the same precaution, and stood switching the flies with her stunted tail. The parson followed her and thankfully grabbed the reins. After several attempts to get up on the wrong side, he led the exacting animal to a log. He removed the veil he wore as a protection from the sticky eye-eating flies, so that Rosey might recognize him as her erstwhile rider. It was at this stage that "flash" Ned Stennard, always with time to kill and a tongue specially designed for the purpose, rode up and gave him lurid instructions and a leg up.

He had come to their remoteness, he told Ned, as they rode along, to hold a service at a grazier's homestead some miles distant. Under Ned's sympathetic guidance he pulled up at the sliprails of a cockey's selection to announce these tidings. It was Ned's brother's place, but Ned, who was not on speaking terms with his sister-in-law, rode on and waited.

A group of half-naked children lay entangled among several kangaroo pups, in a make-believe of shade from a sickly gum-tree. A canvas bag, with a saddle strap defining its long neck, hung from a bough, and the pups were yelping mildly at its contents, and licking the few drops of blood that fell. The parson saw the children rub the swarming flies from their eyes and turn to look at him. An older girl, bare-footed and dressed in a petticoat and old hat, was standing near a fire before the wide opening that served as a doorway to the humpy. She had a long stick, and was employed in permitting an aged billy-goat to bring his nose within an inch of the simmering water in the bucket slung over the fire.

"Are your parents in?" he asked.

"You ain't ole Keogh?" said the girl.

When he admitted that he wasn't, he saw her interest in his personality was gone.

"Are your mother and father in?"

The thirsty billy was sneaking up again to the water, and she let him advance the prescribed limit before she made the jab that she enjoyed so thoroughly. "Mum's gorn ter Tilly Lumber's ter see t' ther kid, and ther rester them's gorn ter ther Circler Dam."

He made known his mission to the girl, but she didn't divide her attention. The water would soon be too hot for the billy to drink, and there was no fun to be got out of the pups. For when she took the salt pork out of the canvas bag and put it in the bucket, they wouldn't try to get it out of boiling water.

Doubtful of his success, the parson rejoined Ned, and along the dusty track they jogged. The parson's part in the dialogue was chiefly remonstrative as to the necessity of Ned's variegated adjectives. And he had frequently to assure the bushman that it would be useless for him to search in his clerical pockets for tobacco, as he didn't smoke.

At the Horse Shoe Bend they overtook hairy Paddy Woods of eighteen withering summers. Paddy was punching and blaspheming a nine-mile day out of his bullocks. These were straining their load along with heads bent close to the dust-padded track, silent, for all the whip-weals, but for a cough to free their mouths and nostrils from dust. Old Rosey, an inveterate yarner, pulled up abruptly; but Paddy, who had his day's work cut out to a minute, gave a voiceless sidelong nod in recognition of the parson's greeting, and went on driving his team. Probably his share of the conversation, mainly catechismal, would have been yea-and-nay nods, but for catching Ned's eye when the parson asked if he were married. Paddy struck an attitude of aged responsibility, and, tipping Ned an intelligent wink, made a pretence of searching through a dusty past, and replied that he thought he was. The parson, giving him the benefit of the doubt, inquired if there were any children for baptism. Paddy, still with an eye on Ned, reckoned that the number of his offspring was uncertain, but promised that as soon as he delivered his load of wool he would have a day's "musterin' an' draftin' an' countin' an' ear-markin'" and send him the returns. Ned's loud laugh and "Good old Paddy" had not the effect on its young-old recipient's well-filled tobacco pouch that he had hoped. The disgusted parson was trying to urge Rosey onward, but Rosey refused to leave her pleasant company till Ned brought his switch across her back.

Ned stayed with Paddy long enough to tell him that, in his opinion, the black-coated parson was "nothin' but a sneakin' Inspector, pokin' an' prowlin' roun' fur ole Keogh" —the lessee of the run, and their common enemy. He added that the green veil he wore over his eyes was a "mast" (mask), but that it didn't deceive him. Tobacco-less Ned tried further to arouse practical admiration from pouch-full Paddy, by adding that he would ride after this disguised Inspector, "pump 'im dry as a blow'd bladder, an' then 'ammer 'ell outer 'im." But even this serious threat against the parson's stock-in-trade had no fruitful result, and, putting his empty pipe back, he galloped after his companion.

As they rode along, the parson in admiration watched the wiry little bushman dexterously winking both eyes to the confusion of the flies, and listened to the substitution of words of his own coinage dropped red-hot into the conversation in place of the sulphurous adjectives. Soon there was but little unknown to Ned's listener of the inner history—and with such additions as contrasted unfavourably with his own—of every selector on this sun-sucked run. In order of infamy Ned placed the lessee first; a good second came the Land Agent in the little township whence this pilgrim parson had come. But this fact was made clear to him, that were the lessee ten times richer, the Land Agent ten times more unscrupulous, were "dummy" selectors occupying every acre, Ned was more than a match for them all.

At a later stage of their journey, when he turned again to the narratives of his cockey brethren, another circumstance stood out. It was only when Ned had exhausted the certainty, probability, and possibility of increase among the mares, cows, ewes, and nannies of his and the other cockies' flocks and herds, that he would descend to the human statistics, and the parson found that impending probability and possibility entered largely into Ned's computation of these.

From time to time they sighted the cockies' humpies, but Ned, intent on making the most of his amazed listener, kept him on the track to his destination by promising to call at all the selections on his way back, and tell them that there was to be a service tomorrow morning. To emphasize his thoroughness, he added, with a wink of bush freemasonry, that he would "on'y tell two sorts—them wot arsts me, an' them wot don't." And this clerical brother, newly initiated into the mysteries of bush craft, could not have found a better messenger. But the wonder expressed in his eyes, as he watched this new labourer in the vineyard cantering briskly away to bear the glad tidings, would have changed to awe could he have heard the varied versions Ned gave to the scattered families as to the need of their being at the grazier's homestead the first thing next day. Moreover, most of the conversation related by Ned as having taken place between the parson and him would have been as new to the former as it was to Ned's audience. For the adjectives with which he flavoured the parson's share proved him to have readily and fluently mastered the lurid bush tongue.

It was shearing time, and, being also the middle of the week, most of the men were away. Those who were at home left their dinners, and came outside to talk to him. A visitor at mealtimes is always met outside the humpy, and the host, drawing a hand across a greasy mouth, leads the way to the nearest log. The women of the bush have little to share, and, nursing the belief that how they live is quite unknown to one another, they have no inclination to entertain a caller. Two of the daily meals consist mainly of sliced damper dipped in a pan of fat, that always hangs over the fire. Mutton at shearing time is a rarity, as the men feed at the sheds. Wild pigs caught and killed by the women make the chief flesh food, but these are often scarce in the dry season.

And in addition Ned was no favourite among the women. This was partly from his being "flash", but more from his reputation for flogging his missus. Ned, moreover, had tried to force his example on the male community by impressing upon them his philosophy, that it was the proper thing to hit a woman every time you met her, since she must either be coming from mischief or going to it. As to his flashness, he considered he had something to be flash about. He had been twice to Sydney; and not only could he spell by ear, but, given an uncertain number of favouring circumstances, he could use a pen to the extent of putting his name to a cheque. Certainly before he would attempt this, Liz, his missus, had to pen up the goats, shut the hut, and, with the dogs and the kids, drive the fowls a mile from the house, and keep them there till Ned fired a gun. Left to himself, Ned would tear out a cheque, lay it on the table, place a block of wood on the bottom edge of the paper, to keep his hand from travelling off it to the table below. Then he had to tie his wrist to the left side of his belt—he was left-handed—in such a manner that his hand could not stray to the foreign region above the cheque, ink the pen with his right hand, and place it in the left. But even then the task was often unaccomplished. Sometimes he would be so intent on trying to keep the *Edward* on the line, that it would run to the end of the paper, excluding the *Stennard*, and, despite Ned's protests anent insufficient space, the bank did not approve of part of the signature being placed on the back of the cheque. When he tried to write small and straight, the result generally seemed satisfactory till a careful analysis showed a letter or so missing. Or just as success seemed probable, his cheque-book would give out or his pen break. It was bad for Liz and her own boy Joey when either of these accidents occurred, for he would fire no gun, and, despite all the perspiring activity of Liz, the kids, and the dogs, some of the fowls would make their way home to roost on the hut when night came. For allowing him to be disturbed "jes as I wus gettin' me 'and in" he would "take it outer" Liz, or, what was worse to her, "outer" Joey.

But on this occasion Ned, ever resourceful and now hungry, refused to be led to a log. His reputation for startling discoveries was against him, but he knew that many of them must have seen him riding past with a black-coated stranger, and he trusted to that to support the story his ingenious imagination had ready for them. Authoritatively he demanded in each case to see the missus. They came ungraciously, but after his dark, bodeful hints as to the necessity of their attending service at the grazier's homestead next day, he was invited inside and a place was cleared for him at the table. Quite recklessly they plied him with pints of tea and damper and dip, sprinkled with salt, and in some extravagant instances with pepper. And Ned took these favours as his due, though he knew he was no favourite.

Flogging and flashness were lost sight of by these anxious women, as they listened to all he had to say. They coaxed him to wait while they searched among the few spare clothes in the gin-cases with hide-hinged lids, for land receipts, marriage lines, letters from Government Departments, registered cattle brands, sheep ear-marks, and every other equipment that protects the poor cockey from a spiteful and revengeful Government, whose sole aim was "ter ketch 'em winkin' " and then forfeit the selection. All of these documents Ned inspected upside down or otherwise, and pronounced with unlegal directness that "a squint et them 'ud fix 'im if thet's wot 'e's smellin' after". He told them to bring them next day. Those of the men who had swapped horses with passing drovers, without the exchange of receipts, were busy all afternoon trumping up witnesses.

II

Next morning the minister was sitting in the rocking-chair on the veranda of the grazier's house. He had a prayer-book in one hand and a handkerchief in the other, with which he lazily disputed the right of the flies to roost on his veil. This gave an undulating motion to the chair which was very soothing after old Rosey's bumping. He saw a pair of brown hands part the awning enclosing the veranda. Then a black head, held in the position of a butting animal, came in view. Free of the screen, the head craned upwards. He saw a flat, shrewd face, with black beady eyes set either side of a bridgeless nose. A wisp of dried grass hung from the wide mouth.

"Sis wants er ride in thet ther cock 'orse yer in," said the mouth, ejecting the grass with considerable force in his direction.

"Sis" had worked her head in by this. She was fair, with nondescript hair and eyes, and she was "chawrin'".

"Wer's ther cock 'orse, Jinny?" she asked, for the chair was not rocking.

"Ridey it an' let 'er see it; an' undo this," commanded Jinny.

"Come round to the front," said the minister mildly, and pointing to the opening opposite the door.

They came in and walked up to him, with hoods hanging by the strings down their backs.

"Have you come alone?"

"The ether uns er comin'. Me an' Sis giv' 'em ther slip; we didn' wanter 'ump ther dash kid."

"How far have you walked?"

"Yer parst our place yesserday mornin'. Didn' yer see me an' ther billy? Gosh, we nigh bust oursels at ther way yer legs stuck out. Fust I thort yer wus ole Keogh. Yer rides jes' like er Chinymun." The dark one did all the talking.

"Our Sis wants er ride in this," she continued. She gave the chair a lurch that sent the parson's feet in the air. To avoid the threatened repetition he gripped both sides and planted his feet firmly on the boards.

The younger one poked a stem of dried grass from her mouth through the mesh of the veil in a line with his left ear. Thoroughly routed, he sprang up, and the elder child leapt in.

" 'Ere they cum, Jinny," warned Sis.

Jinny peeped through the awning. "So they is. You gammon ter them we ain't cum, w'en they arsts yer," she said to the parson, "an' we'll sneak roun' ther back. Eh, Sis?"

Mammy and Daddy—commonly called "Jyne" and "Alick" even by their offspring—came in with four children, all younger than Jinny and Sis. Jyne carried the youngest straddled across her hip.

The most pronounced feature of Jyne's face was her mouth, and it seemed proud of its teeth, especially of the top row. Without any apparent effort, the last tooth there was always visible. She was a great power in the bush, being styled by the folk themselves "Rabbit Ketcher", which, translated, means midwife. And the airs Jyne gave herself were justifiable, for she was the only "Rabbit Ketcher" this side of the township. To bring a qualified midwife from civilization would have represented a crippling expenditure to these cockies. Jyne's moderate fees were usually four-legged.

"D'y ter yous," said Alick, blinking his bungy eyes, and smiling good-naturedly at the parson and at the grazier and his wife. He sat down without removing his hat. Jyne's teeth saluted them but without any good nature. Jinny and Sis sneaked in behind their mother.

"You young tinkers," cried Jyne, "tyke this chile this minute." Her voice, despite the size of her mouth, came through her nose. She put the baby on the floor, and, taking off her hood, mopped her face with the inside of her print dress.

"We wus lookin' fer you an' Alick," said Jinny to her mother, and winking at the parson.

"Yes, you wus—with ther 'ook," answered Jyne.

Without further introduction she slewed her head to one side, shut one eye knowingly, and said to the staring minister, "Ther ain't a wink about Jinny."

The unblinking daughter instantly offered an illustration of her wakefulness. "Yer orter seen me an' gran'dad th' ether mornin'. 'E wus milkin' ther nannies, an' ther billy you seen 'e wus jes close agen 'im. I sneaks up to ther billy an' gives 'im er jab. Lawr ter see 'im rush et ole Alex an' bunt 'im! 'E'd er killed th' ole feller on'y fer me. Wou'dn' 'e, mum?"

"Yer a bol' gal," said mum in a proud voice.

The bewildered minister, to turn the conversation, took a vase of wild-flowers.

"They belong to the lily tribe, I think," said the hostess. "They are bulbous."

"Wile hunyions," sniffed Jyne, making no attempt to conceal her contempt for this cur of a woman, who thought so much of herself that she always brought a nurse from town.

Then came Alick's brother, "Flash" Ned; they were as unlike as brothers sometimes are. Ned greeted the parson with bush familiarity. He had his hat on one side, and was wearing a silk Sydney coat that reached to his heels. He was followed by Liz with their family of five. Joey stayed outside, and from time to time dexterously located his step-father. He was Liz's child by an early marriage—at least, she always said she had been married.

Perched on Liz's head was a draggled hat that a month ago had been snow-white. This also was one of Ned's Sydney purchases. It was the first time Liz had worn it, but she and the children had overhauled it many times and tried it on. This privilege had been extended to all the women whose curiosity and envy had brought them to Liz's place. Jinny had called on her way to church, and the missing end of the white feather, after being licked of its ticklesomeness, was now in her safe keeping.

Jyne, catching sight of Joey, invited him inside. But the boy, at a warning glance from his mother, slunk further back. He had run in the wrong horse for his step-father that morning, and was evading a threatened hiding that was to remove both skin and hair. Liz would gladly have taken the hiding herself in place of Joey, but her inter-ference, as she knew to her cost, would mean one for her-self without saving the boy.

But for all this Liz thought she was fairly happy. For it was not every day that Ned tried to sign a cheque or that the sheep got boxed, or that his horse refused to be caught. Nor did it always rain when he wanted it fine. Things did not go wrong every day, and he did not beat her or Joey unless they did. A pound of lollies for her and the kids from a dealer's cart when one came round, would make her think him the best husband in the world.

There was between Jyne and Ned the opposition that is instinctive between commanding spirits. Liz yielded obedi-ence first to Ned then to Jyne.

"Ow's Polly!" inquired Liz, her countenance showing the gravity of the question.

"Arst 'im," snarled Jyne, baring her fangs and looking at uneasy shuffling Alick. "Makin' 'er dror three casts er worter ten mile, an' 'er thet way. Wil' pigs eatin' 'er as I cum along."

"No!" said Liz, though she had known it all yesterday. News of such catastrophes soon spread in the bush.

"Better corl me a liar at onct," snapped Jyne.

Next to arrive were Jyne's mother and Alick's father, both of whom lived with Jyne. The old woman rode on a horse astride a man's saddle. The old man led it. She had Jyne's mouth, or rather Jyne had hers, but the teeth were gone. The old man greeted the parson reverently, blew with his breath on the seat, and wiped it carefully with the handkerchief he had taken from his hat. Even then before sitting he raised the tails of the coat he had been married in so long ago. Until Ned's Sydney purchase his had been the only decorative coat in the district.

Tilly and Jim Lumber, with their ten-days-old baby, followed. Jim was the champion concertina player and bullock driver in the district. He came as the representative of the several families across the creek, whom energetic Ned had rounded up the day before. He had been chosen by them for his size and strength to do battle on their behalf. Ned's effort to frighten those women whose husbands were away shearing into the necessity of attending service had over-reached itself, and they had been afraid to come. But they had entrusted their precious documents to Jim's powerful keeping. He had his own registered brand tied up in a spotted handkerchief. This he dropped with a clank beside him as he sat sheepishly and gingerly on the edge of a chair. He was over six feet, but he sat with his head almost between his knees, till he resembled a quadruped. His shirt front bulged like a wallet with his clients' papers. He slyly took stock of those assembled. Spry little Tilly got the credit of having done all the courting. Even after marriage she had always done his share of the talking.

"Ow's ther kiddy maroo?" said Alick to Jim, lisping from

the size of the plug he had just bitten. He had a fatherly interest in all Jyne's "rabbit ketchin' ".

Jim, who never used his voice except to drive his bullocks, answered with a subterranean laugh.

"Noo bit er flesh," said Ned, nodding at the baby.

"Ow's Polly this mornin'?" gravely inquired Tilly, as she took a seat near Jyne.

"Ah, poor Polly," quavered Jyne's mother, and sparing Jyne by telling of Polly's untimely end.

"Well, I'm blest; what a lorse!" said the sympathetic Tilly. She repeated a well-known story of the bu'stin' of a poley cow last year.

Jyne took the baby, and began to rate the mother mildly for "walkin' seven mile ser soon", but Jyne's mother interposed with a recital of "wot I dun w'en Jun" (John) "wur two days old." John was present, fully six feet of him, grinning with a mouth bigger than Jyne's, but mercifully hidden by a straggled moustache.

However, Jyne was not to be outdone even by her own mother, and the narrative of her last, assisted in many minor details by Jinny, aged eleven, left little to be desired in the way of hardihood.

Liz kept her teething baby respectfully silent by industriously rubbing its lower gum with a dirty thumb. She expressed her surprise at Jyne's phenomenal endurance by little clicks of the tongue, shakes of the head, and other signs indicative of admiration and astonishment. When Jyne finished, she began eagerly on an experience of her own. "Well, w'en I wus took with Drary" (short for Adrarian) "think I could fin' ther sissers?"

Jyne, who knew that the recital of a daring feat was coming, inquired, "W'en yer wus took with Joey?"

"No," said Liz, stopping short with a nervous click in her voice, and looking at Ned.

The next item was ventriloquizing by Jyne per medium

of Tilly's uneasy baby. "My mammy, she sez, yer dot me all o'a hoo, she sez. No wunny, she sez, me can't keep goody, she sez, 'ith me cosey all o'a hoo, she sez." She had been examining the baby's undergear, and at this stage her tone of baby banter suddenly changed to one of professional horror. "My Gawd, Tilly!" she cried, the drooping corners of her mouth nearly covering her upper teeth. "Look w'er 'er little belly-bands is—nearly un'er 'er arms," she explained, probably to the company, but looking directly at the clergyman. And, with true professional acumen, she intimated that had she not been on the spot, an intricate part of the little one's anatomy in another minute would " 'a bust out a bleedin' an' not all ther doctors in ther worl' couldn' astoppt it."

The minister was very busy, meanwhile, blushing and getting his books in order, and with his congregation of ten adults and eighteen children he began, "Dearly beloved brethren—"

Jim Lumber gripped his bullock brand, took a swift look at him and turned to Tilly. It had been settled between them that she was to do the talking. Alick, who, despite his father's efforts to enlighten him as to the nature of a church service, and encouraged by Jyne's remark that "they'd eat nothin' ", had also brought his valuable documents in his shirt front, thrust in a groping hand.

For a few minutes the adults listened and watched intently, but the gentle voice of the parson, and his nervous manner, soon convinced them that they had nothing to fear from him. Ned had been "pokin' borak" at them again; they added it to the long score they owed him.

The children wandered about the room. Jinny and Sis invited their little sister to "Cum an' see ther pooty picters in the man's book," and they assisted the minister to turn over the leaves of his Bible.

Alick's father, who was from the North of Ireland, and,

for all his forty years in the bush, had not lost his reverence for the cloth, bade his grand-daughters beseechingly to "quet", whereupon Jinny showed him quite two inches of inky tongue. Ink was a commodity unknown in Jinny's home, and all the unknown is edible to the bush child.

"Woman!" he said, appealing to Jinny's mother, "whybut you bid 'er to quet?"

"You orter be in er glars' ban' box w'er ther ain't no children; thet's w'er you orter be," answered Jyne.

He beckoned to one straggler, a girl of six, with Alick's face, who came to him promptly and sat on his knee.

Presently her brown hand stroked his old cheek. "Gran'-dad," she said.

"Choot, darlin'," he whispered, reverently.

The child looked at him wonderingly. "I says you's gran'-dad, she repeated, "not ole Alick."

He laid his white head on hers.

"Gran'-dad, ole Tommy Tolbit's dead."

Turning his glistening face to Liz in momentary forgetfulness, he said solemnly, "The knowledge of this chile!"

"Ole Talbert" had been dead for two years, and the knowledgeable child had been surprising him so, at least twice a week.

"We have erred and strayed from Thy ways like lost sheep," murmured the minister.

The smaller children wandered in and out of the bedrooms, carrying their spoils with them. But Jinny and Sis had drawn the now disabled rocking-chair up to the window, and were busy poking faces at two of Liz's children, who were standing on the couch inside. One of these made a vicious smack with a hair-brush at Jinny's tongue, flattened against the glass. The ensuing crash stopped even the parson for a moment.

Bravely he began again. He paused occasionally for a sudden subterranean laugh to cease or to put one book after another on the shelf behind him out of the children's reach. Just as he read the last line of the Te Deum, "Oh Lord in Thee have I trusted, let me never be confounded," one of Liz's children tugged at his trousers, with a muzzled request that his teeth might be freed from a square of pink soap. Another offered to the baby Liz was nursing a pincushion she brought from the bedroom.

"Jyne," called Jinny from the veranda, " 'ere cums young Tommy Tolbit by 'isself. You wus right, Jyne; she ain't cummin'!"

Even Jyne's gums gleamed; she looked triumphantly at Alick her husband, at Liz, then at all but Ned.

In shambled Tommy, moist and panting. He had been a drover, and had recently taken up a selection on the run. He was a bridegroom of a month's standing. His missus had been a servant at one of the hotels in the township.

"Made a start!" he remarked. His voice gave the impression that he did not mind their not waiting for him.

"Missus ain't comin'?" inquired Alick, trying to atone to Jyne for overloading Polly.

"Not ter day," said the bridegroom, but his voice intimated that in all probability she would have been able to come tomorrow.

"No!" said Jyne, putting him under fire, and trying to keep the crow out of her voice.

"Ain't very well, is she? Didn' eat a very 'earty break-fuss this mornin'?" And a further remark suggested that even if the meal had been hearty, the usual process of assimilation had not taken place.

"Ow's Polly?" he inquired.

"Cooked," said Jyne, instantly diverted.

"Go on!" said the bridegroom, with well feigned astonishment. His breathless and perspiring state had been caused by his "going on" to capture one of the wild suckers that had been eating Polly.

"Let us pray," said the minister. His host, hostess, and Alick's father knelt, but the rest sat as usual.

The knowledgeable child, considering the grandfather's position an invitation to mount, climbed on his back. Making a bridle of the handkerchief round the old fellow's neck, and digging two heels into his sides, she talked horse to him. The protesting old man bucked vigorously, but it was no easy task to throw her.

The clergyman gave out his text, and the sermon began.

Jyne's children commenced to complain of being " 'ungry" and a fair-sized damper was taken from a pillow-slip. This, together with two tin tots and a bottle of goat's milk, was given to Jinny and she was told to do "ther sharin' ".

The hostess asked Jyne in a whisper to send them to the veranda, and for a time there was comparative quiet. Such interruptions as "Jinny won't gimme nun, Arnie" (Auntie) from Liz's children being checked by Jyne with "Go an' play an' doan' 'ave ser much gab, like yer father."

"Thet greedy wretch uv er Jinny is guzzlin' all ther milk inter 'er, Jyne," from her own children, was appeased by her promise to "break ther young faggit's back w'en I get 'ome."

There was a wail of anguished hunger from Liz's empty children that aroused paternal sympathy in Ned. "Sep me Gord," he said, "some wimmen is like cows. They'll give ther own calf a suck, but if anyone else's calf cums anigh 'em they lif' their leg an' kick it ter blazes."

Jyne tossed her head and, with a derisive laugh, expressed the opinion that "It 'ed fit sum people better if ther munny wasted in buyin' flash coats an' rediclus 'ats wus spent in flour bags."

For a short space only the voice of the preacher sounded, as, in studied stoicism, he pursued his thankless task.

Occasionally they looked at him to see " 'oo 'e wus speakin' ter", but finding nothing directly personal, even this attention ceased.

Liz leant across to Tilly Lumber and asked, "Fowl layin'?"

"Ketch 'em er layin' et Chrissermus."

Ned told how he had brought home a number of law books from Sydney, and that he and an old man he had picked up "wus readin' 'em". It was his intention to absorb such an amount of knowledge that all he would have to do with the lessee of the run—an ex-barrister—would be to put him in a bail. What would follow was graphically illustrated by Ned's dropping his head, gripping an imaginary bucket between his knees, and opening and shutting his hands in rhythmic up and down movements. Some of his audience, remembering his threats and warnings against the parson, thought this pantomime must have an ominous meaning for the preacher.

But sceptical Jyne was not impressed. "Upon me soul," she said, "sum people is the biggest lyin' blowers that ever cockt er lip."

Alick, always for peace, stepped into the breach. "Comin' along jes' now," he said, shifting his plug of tobacco from one side to the other, and aiming at the flies in the fireplace with the juice, "we 'as a yarn with Mick Byrnes. 'E 'as ther luck of er lousy calf. 'E sez 'e got eightpence orl roun' fer 'ees kangaroo-skins. Damned if I can."

"Now a good plan 'ed be," said Ned, "ter get a good lot, sen' 'em down ter them Sydney blokes. Slip down yerself, go ter ther sale, don' let on 'oo yer are, an' run 'em up like blazes. Thet's wot I'll do with my wool nex' year."

This plan seemed commendable to Alick. "By Goey," he said, his mild eyes blinking.

Jyne never, on any occasion, showed the slightest interest or attention when Ned was speaking, unless to sniff and

K

lay bare her bottom teeth, but here she remarked, "Sum people 'ud keep runnin' ter Sydney till 'e 'asen' er penny ter fly with."

"If sum people with ser much jawr, an' er mouth es big es 'er torn pocket, belonged ter me," said Ned, "I'd smash 'er ugly jawr."

Jyne slewed hers to an awful angle in his direction. "I'd like ter see yer try it."

A look of agony came into the eyes of the grazier's wife as she heard the door of the dining-room open. The children were so quiet, that she knew they were up to mischief.

She heard Jinny's hoarse whisper, "Orl of yez wait an' I'll bring yer sumsin'." On the dining-room table was the cold food prepared for the clergyman's dinner. She looked across at her husband with dumb entreaty. He, with eyes devoutly on the carpet, was listening intently to Ned's account of how he nearly made the squatter take a "sugar doodle" (back somersault) when he heard that he had been to Sydney.

" 'Day Keogh,' sez I.

" ' 'Oo 'ave I ther 'oner of speakin' ter?' sez 'e.

" 'Mr Stennard,' I sez.

" 'Oh indeed,' 'e sez, 'very 'appy ter make yer acquaintance, Mr Stennard, Esquire,' 'e sez.

" 'Never mind no blarsted acquaintance,' I sez, 'w'en are yer goin' ter take yer flamin' jumbucks orf my lan'?' I sez.

" 'Your lan',' 'e sez, 'I didn' know you 'ad any lan' about 'ere,' 'e sez.

" 'Oh, didn' yer,' I sez, 'you ner ther Lan' Agent won' frighten me orf,' I sez, 'gammonin' I'm on er reserve,' sez I, 'I've paid me deposit, an' I've been ter Sydney,' I sez, 'I put me name ter a cheque,' sez I, 'an'—' "

Jyne ceased sniffing, to laugh long and loudly. "Gawd, eh!" she said, with her eyes on the ceiling and apparently appealing to the flies. "Wot 'erbout sech game-cocks bullyin' w'en we fust kem out 'ere?"

Ned went hastily out at the front door "ter squint at ther jumbucks", three miles away. Joey, who had been peering round that door, now appeared at the back.

"Come in, Joey," snorted Jyne. "No one ain't game ter 'it yer w'en I'm 'ere."

The minister still preached, but he had only old Alick for a listener.

The hostess's mental picture of Jinny "sharin'" her dinner for three among that voracious brood was distracting. Only the fear of suffering in the clergyman's mind as one of "them" kept her to her seat. She could give the sermon no attention, but listened to Sis licking her fingers, and wondered if it was the vinegar or the wine that caused Jinny's cough. Presently Jinny set that doubt at rest by coming in odorous, and with the front of her dress wine-stained.

"Little 'un snoozin'!" Jinny remarked, lurching giddily towards her to merrily twirl her fist in the snoozer. The snoozer's mother wondered if they had shut the dining-room door. Soon the noise of the fowls scattering the crockery told her they had not.

"Thum busted fowls is eatin' orl yer dinner," said Jinny dreamily.

" 'Unt 'em out an' shet ther door," said sympathetic Jyne.

"You go, Sis, I'm tired." Jinny laid her giddy head on the floor, and went to sleep.

"Liz," said Jyne, maliciously, for she immediately grudged Sis's efforts to chase the fowls out of the dining-room. "Wot's thet there flower?" pointing to the vase.

"Wile huniyon," said Liz, promptly.

"Er, is it? Thet's orl yer know. Thet's a bulbers, thet is. Thet's ther noo name fer it." She looked at the grazier's wife and laughed ironically.

"Bulbers! yer goat," said Liz, laughing dutifully.

The sermon was over, and the worried minister began the christening.

The naming of the hostess's baby was plain sailing. He then drew towards him a child of about two years, and asked, "What is this child's name?"

"Adrarian," said Liz. An old shepherd reading to her a love-story had so pronounced the hero's name. It staggered the minister, until his hostess spelt "Adrian".

"What is its age?"

"About two year."

This was too vague for him, and he pressed for dates. But for these dwellers in the bush the calendar had no significance. The mother thought it might be in November. "Cos it wus shearin', an' I'd ter keep Teddy at 'ome ter do ther work." Teddy was "about ten". From these uncertainties the clergyman had to supply the dates for his official returns to the Government.

"But Lawd," as Jyne remarked to ease his perplexity, "wot did it matter fer a brat of er boy?" She had a family of six, and all were girls.

There was much the same difficulty with all the others, an exception being Tilly Lumber's baby of under a fortnight. A cowardly look came into the minister's eyes as he turned to this grotesque atom already in the short coat stage. He remembered Jyne's awful discovery of a little while back, and shirked the duty of holding it even for a moment.

The christening was a matter that had some personal interest for the elders, and they grouped round the minister. Bridegroom Tommy, striking the mossy back of Alick's old father, suggested that he and Jyne's mother should get spliced, and he expressed the opinion of the fruitfulness of such union within record time as a set-off dig at Jyne.

She instantly balanced matters between herself and the

incautiously smiling Liz and the laughing unfilial Ned. "Stop scratchin' yer 'ed, miss; anyone 'ud think there wus anythink in it," she said to Liz's eldest girl, who was brushing the christening water from her hair. Ned's stepson she invited to come nearer, and tell her who had blackened his poor eye. She advised the silent lad "ter get a waddy ther nex' time anyone bigger'n yer goes ter 'it yer". And she gave him directions by twirling an imaginary waddy swiftly, its circuit suddenly diverting in a line with Ned's skull.

It was long past noon when the ceremony was ended. The minister drained his glass of water, mopped his face, and heaved a deep sigh. As the whole congregation still sat on, he gave them a hint that "church" was out, and their presence no longer required. He spoke with a show of concern of how very hot they would find the walk home, and to further emphasize his meaning, he shook hands with all the adults, and walked to the veranda. Without the slightest concern they sat on, listening intently to the sounds the hostess made in trying to scrape together a meal for the clergyman. Apparently they all meant to stay the day.

The grazier's wife appeared for a moment to beckon him to go round the house into the dining-room. He sat down to the remains of the dinner the children had left.

At that moment Jinny, who had been awakened for the christening, looked round the door. "Our Sis wants ter know w'en's 'er supper's goin' ter be!" she said.

This perhaps was an acknowledgement that Sis had already dined.

The Chosen Vessel

SHE laid the stick and her baby on the grass while she untied the rope that tethered the calf. The length of the rope separated them. The cow was near the calf, and both were lying down. Feed along the creek was plentiful, and every day she found a fresh place to tether it, since tether it she must, for if she did not, it would stray with the cow out on the plain. She had plenty of time to go after it, but then there was baby; and if the cow turned on her out on the plain, and she with baby—she had been a town girl and was afraid of the cow, but she did not want the cow to know it. She used to run at first when it bellowed its protest against the penning up of its calf. This satisfied the cow, also the calf, but the woman's husband was angry, and called her—the noun was cur. It was he who forced her to run and meet the advancing cow, brandishing a stick, and uttering threatening words till the enemy turned and ran. "That's the way!" the man said, laughing at her white face. In many things he was worse than the cow, and she wondered if the same rule would apply to the man, but she was not one to provoke skirmishes even with the cow.

It was early for the calf to go "to bed"—nearly an hour earlier than usual; but she had felt so restless all day. Partly because it was Monday, and the end of the week that would bring her and baby the companionship of its father, was so far off. He was a shearer, and had gone to his shed before daylight that morning. Fifteen miles as the crow flies separated them.

There was a track in front of the house, for it had once been a wine shanty, and a few travellers passed along at intervals. She was not afraid of horsemen; but swagmen, going to, or worse, coming from the dismal, drunken little township, a day's journey beyond, terrified her. One had called at the house today, and asked for tucker.

Ah! that was why she had penned up the calf so early! She feared more from the look of his eyes, and the gleam of his teeth, as he watched her newly awakened baby beat its impatient fists upon her covered breasts, than from the knife that was sheathed in the belt at his waist.

She had given him bread and meat. Her husband, she told him, was sick. She always said that when she was alone, and a swagman came, and she had gone in from the kitchen to the bedroom, and asked questions and replied to them in the best man's voice she could assume. Then he had asked to go into the kitchen to boil his billy, but she gave him tea, and he drank it on the wood-heap. He had walked round and round the house, and there were cracks in some places, and after the last time he had asked for tobacco. She had none to give him, and he had grinned, because there was a broken clay pipe near the wood-heap where he stood, and if there were a man inside, there ought to have been tobacco. Then he asked for money, but women in the bush never have money.

At last he had gone, and she, watching through the cracks, saw him when about a quarter of a mile away, turn and look back at the house. He had stood so for some moments with a pretence of fixing his swag, and then, apparently satisfied, moved to the left towards the creek.

The creek made a bow round the house, and when he came to it she lost sight of him. Hours after, watching intently for signs of smoke, she saw the man's dog chasing some sheep that had gone to the creek for water, and saw it slink back suddenly, as if the man had called it.

More than once she thought of taking her baby and going to her husband. But in the past, when she had dared to speak of the dangers to which her loneliness exposed her, he had taunted and sneered at her. She need not flatter herself, he had coarsely told her, that anybody would want to run away with her.

Long before nightfall she placed food on the kitchen table, and beside it laid the big brooch that had been her mother's. It was the only thing of value that she had. And she left the kitchen door wide open.

The doors inside she securely fastened. Beside the bolt in the back one she drove in the steel and scissors; against it she piled the table and the stools. Underneath the lock of the front door she forced the handle of the spade, and the blade between the cracks in the flooring boards. Then the prop-stick, cut into lengths, held the top, as the spade held the middle. The windows were little more than portholes; she had nothing to fear through them.

She ate a few mouthfuls of food and drank a cup of milk. But she lighted no fire, and when night came, no candle, but crept with her baby to bed.

What woke her? The wonder was that she had slept— she had not meant to. But she was young, very young. Perhaps the shrinking of the galvanized roof—yet hardly, since that was so usual. Something had set her heart beating wildly; but she lay quite still, only she put her arm over her baby. Then she had both round it, and she prayed, "Little baby, little baby, don't wake!"

The moon's rays shone on the front of the house, and she saw one of the open cracks, quite close to where she lay, darken with a shadow. Then a protesting growl reached her; and she could fancy she heard the man turn hastily. She plainly heard the thud of something striking the dog's ribs, and the long flying strides of the animal as it howled and ran. Still watching, she saw the shadow darken every crack along the wall. She knew by the sounds that the man was trying every standpoint that might help him to see in; but how much he saw she could not tell. She thought of many things she might do to deceive him into the idea that she was not alone. But the sound of her voice would wake baby, and she dreaded that as though it were the only danger that threatened her. So she prayed, "Little baby, don't wake, don't cry!"

Stealthily the man crept about. She knew he had his boots off, because of the vibration that his feet caused as he walked along the veranda to gauge the width of the little window in her room, and the resistance of the front door.

Then he went to the other end, and the uncertainty of what he was doing became unendurable. She had felt safer, far safer, while he was close, and she could watch and listen. She felt she must watch, but the great fear of wakening baby again assailed her. She suddenly recalled that one of the slabs on that side of the house had shrunk in length as well as in width, and had once fallen out. It was held in position only by a wedge of wood underneath. What if he should discover that! The uncertainty increased her terror. She prayed as she gently raised herself with her little one in her arms, held tightly to her breast.

She thought of the knife, and shielded her child's body with her hands and arms. Even its little feet she covered with its white gown, and baby never murmured—it liked to be held so. Noiselessly she crossed to the other side, and stood where she could see and hear, but not be seen. He was trying every slab, and was very near to that with the wedge under it. Then she saw him find it; and heard the sound of the knife as bit by bit he began to cut away the wooden support.

She waited motionless, with her baby pressed tightly to her, though she knew that in another few minutes this man with the cruel eyes, lascivious mouth, and gleaming knife, would enter. One side of the slab tilted; he had only to cut away the remaining little end, when the slab, unless he held it, would fall outside.

She heard his jerked breathing as it kept time with the cuts of the knife, and the brush of his clothes as he rubbed the wall in his movements, for she was so still and quiet, that she did not even tremble. She knew when he ceased, and wondered why. She stood well concealed; she knew he could not see her, and that he would not fear if he did, yet she heard him move cautiously away. Perhaps he expected the slab to fall. Still his motive puzzled her, and she moved even closer, and bent her body the better to listen. Ah! what sound was that? "Listen! Listen!" she bade her heart —her heart that had kept so still, but now bounded with tumultuous throbs that dulled her ears. Nearer and nearer came the sounds, till the welcome thud of a horse's hoof rang out clearly.

"Oh, God! Oh, God! Oh, God!" she cried, for they were very close before she could make sure. She turned to the door, and with her baby in her arms tore frantically at its bolts and bars.

Out she darted at last, and running madly along, saw the horseman beyond her in the distance. She called to him in Christ's name, in her babe's name, still flying like the wind with the speed that deadly peril gives. But the distance grew greater and greater between them, and when she reached the creek her prayers turned to wild shrieks, for there crouched the man she feared, with outstretched arms that caught her as she fell. She knew he was offering terms if she ceased to struggle and cry for help, though louder and louder did she cry for it, but it was only when the man's hand gripped her throat, that the cry of "Murder" came from her lips. And when she ceased, the startled curlews took up the awful sound, and flew shrieking over the horseman's head.

"By God!" said the boundary rider, "it's been a dingo right enough! Eight killed up here, and there's more down in the creek—a ewe and a lamb, I'll bet; and the lamb's alive!" And he shut out the sky with his hand, and watched the crows that were circling round and round, nearing the earth one moment, and the next shooting skywards. By that he knew the lamb must be alive; even a dingo will spare a lamb sometimes.

Yes, the lamb was alive, and after the manner of lambs of its kind did not know its mother when the light came. It had sucked the still warm breasts, and laid its little head on her bosom, and slept till the morn. Then, when it looked at the swollen disfigured face, it wept and would have crept away, but for the hand that still clutched its little gown. Sleep was nodding its golden head and swaying its small body, and the crows were close, so close, to the mother's wide-open eyes, when the boundary rider galloped down.

"Jesus Christ!" he said, covering his eyes. He told afterwards how the little child held out its arms to him, and how he was forced to cut its gown that the dead hand held.

It was election time, and as usual the priest had selected a candidate. His choice was so obviously in the interests of the squatter, that Peter Hennessey's reason, for once in his life, had over-ridden superstition, and he had dared promise his vote to another. Yet he was uneasy, and every time he woke in the night (and it was often) he heard the murmur of his mother's voice. It came through the partition, or under the door. If through the partition, he knew she was praying in her bed; but when the sounds came under the door, she was on her knees before the little altar in the corner that enshrined the statue of the Blessed Virgin and Child.

"Mary, Mother of Christ! save my son! Save him!" prayed she in the dairy as she strained and set the evening's milking. "Sweet Mary! for the love of Christ, save him!" The grief in her old face made the morning meal so bitter, that to avoid her he came late to his dinner. It made him so cowardly, that he could not say goodbye to her, and when night fell on the eve of the election day, he rode off secretly.

He had thirty miles to ride to the township to record his vote. He cantered briskly along the great stretch of plain that had nothing but stunted cottonbush to play shadow to the full moon, which glorified a sky of earliest spring. The bruised incense of the flowering clover rose up to him, and the glory of the night appealed vaguely to his imagination, but he was preoccupied with his present act of revolt.

Vividly he saw his mother's agony when she would find him gone. At that moment, he felt sure, she was praying.

"Mary! Mother of Christ!" He repeated the invocation, half unconsciously. And suddenly, out of the stillness, came Christ's name to him—called loudly in despairing accents.

"For Christ's sake! Christ's sake! Christ's sake!" called the voice. Good Catholic that he had been, he crossed himself before he dared to look back. Gliding across a ghostly patch of pipe-clay, he saw a white-robed figure with a babe clasped to her bosom.

All the superstitious awe of his race and religion swayed his brain. The moonlight on the gleaming clay was a "heavenly light" to him, and he knew the white figure not for flesh and blood, but for the Virgin and Child of his mother's prayers. Then, good Catholic that once more he was, he put spurs to his horse's sides and galloped madly away.

His mother's prayers were answered.

Hennessey was the first to record his vote—for the priest's candidate. Then he sought the priest at home, but found that he was out rallying the voters. Still, under the influence of his blessed vision, Hennessey would not go near the public-houses, but wandered about the outskirts of the town for hours, keeping apart from the townspeople, and fasting as penance. He was subdued and mildly ecstatic, feeling as a repentant chastened child, who awaits only the kiss of peace.

And at last, as he stood in the graveyard crossing himself with reverent awe, he heard in the gathering twilight the roar of many voices crying the name of the victor at the election. It was well with the priest.

Again Hennessey sought him. He sat at home, the housekeeper said, and led him into the dimly-lighted study. His seat was immediately opposite a large picture, and as the housekeeper turned up the lamp, once more the face of the Madonna and Child looked down on him, but this time silently, peacefully. The half-parted lips of the Virgin were smiling with compassionate tenderness; her eyes seemed to beam with the forgiveness of an earthly mother for her erring but beloved child.

He fell on his knees in adoration. Transfixed, the wondering priest stood, for, mingled with the adoration, "My Lord and my God!" was the exaltation, "And hast Thou chosen me?"

"What is it, Peter?" said the priest.

"Father," he answered reverently, and with loosened tongue he poured forth the story of his vision.

"Great God!" shouted the priest, "and you did not stop to save her! Have you not heard?"

Many miles further down the creek a man kept throwing
an old cap into a waterhole. The dog would bring it out
and lay it on the opposite side to where the man stood, but
would not allow the man to catch him, though it was
only to wash the blood of the sheep from his mouth and
throat, for the sight of blood made the man tremble.

Katharine Susannah Prichard

COONARDOO

'Recognised as a novel that broke important ground,
Coonardoo was published to critical acclaim as well as public outrage . . .
Sixty years later, it continues to make uncomfortable reading, and the
challenge that Katharine Susannah Prichard throws to white
Australia — that we come to terms with Aboriginal Australia
or perish — still comes in on target.'
DRUSILLA MODJESKA, from the Introduction

Coonardoo tells the story of a young Aboriginal woman who is trained
from childhood to be the housekeeper at Wytaliba station and to look
after its owner, Hugh Watt. The love that develops between them can
never be acknowledged in their world and so becomes a deeply
destructive force.

This tough, uncompromising novel set on the edges of the desert is a
landmark in the creative exploration of black/white relations in this
country, and makes unforgettable reading.

THE ROARING NINETIES

'*The mining industry might make for wealth and power for a few men
and women, but the many would always be smashed and battered beneath
its giant treads, as the batteries were breaking stone, tonight . . . She could not
escape from her place beneath those treads, Sally knew . . .* '

In the spring of 1892 gold fever swept Western Australia like a forest fire.
Prospectors, miners storekeepers, brothel keepers and speculators
swarmed over the vast, unknown back-country of the West, prepared to
risk all for the elusive chance of gold.

In this enthralling story of friendship and love, of success and failure,
of violence and death, of tremendous riches and terrible poverty, Sally
Gough, tough and determined, braves hardship and danger on the
goldfield. *The Roaring Nineties*, a classic tale of pioneering Australia, is the
first in Katharine Susannah Prichard's epic trilogy of novels featuring this
remarkable character.

HAXBY'S CIRCUS

Haxby's Circus, the 'lightest, brightest little show on earth', is the story of a small family circus, its travels through outback New South Wales and Victoria, and the relationships that both flourish and wither under its big top. Among its characters are the proprietor, Dan Haxby, whose devotion to the maxim that 'the show must go on' overrides any concern for his family's welfare; his daughter Gina, the bareback rider whose tragic accident reveals a courageous spirit in command of her fate; and the circus dwarf Rocca, who shows Gina how to transform her liability into art.

Now a major Australian theatrical production

WORKING BULLOCKS

'Then the team swung out from the bush, turning into the track,
sunlight striking down through young green of the redgum and jarrah saplings,
splashing the big red and white bullocks in the lead. Red, tawny, black, and
white backs of the beasts moved slowly, with rippling sway, against
the lighted and shadowy depths of the forest.'

Set in the early 1920s, *Working Bullocks* uses this magnificent image of harnessed power to tell the passionate story of the men who work the bullock teams and the women who live with them in the great Karrie forests of Western Australia.

Both political allegory and love story, this classic novel remains a highlight of Katharine Susannah Prichard's literary achievement.